A Book of Old Ballads

Beverly Nichols

A BOOK OF OLD BALLADS

ACKNOWLEDGMENTS

The thanks and acknowledgments of the publishers are due to the following: to Messrs. B. Feldman & Co., 125 Shaftesbury Avenue, W.C. 2, for "It's a Long Way to Tipperary"; to Mr. Rudyard Kipling and Messrs. Methuen & Co. for "Mandalay" from *Barrack Room Ballads*; and to the Executors of the late Oscar Wilde for "The Ballad of Reading Gaol."

"The Earl of Mar's Daughter", "The Wife of Usher's Well", "The Three Ravens", "Thomas the Rhymer", "Clerk Colvill", "Young Beichen", "May Collin", and "Hynd Horn" have been reprinted from *English and Scottish Ballads*, edited by Mr. G. L. Kittredge and the late Mr. F. J. Child, and published by the Houghton Mifflin Company.

The remainder of the ballads in this book, with the exception of "John Brown's Body", are from *Percy's Reliques*, Volumes I and II.

CONTENTS

LIST OF ILLUSTRATIONS

FOREWORD

By Beverley Nichols

These poems are the very essence of the British spirit. They are, to literature, what the bloom of the heather is to the Scot, and the smell of the sea to the Englishman. All that is beautiful in the old word "patriotism" . . . a word which, of late, has been twisted to such ignoble purposes . . . is latent in these gay and full-blooded measures.

But it is not only for these reasons that they are so valuable to the modern spirit. It is rather for their tonic qualities that they should be prescribed in 1934. The post-war vintage of poetry is the thinnest and the most watery that England has ever produced. But here, in these ballads, are great draughts of poetry which have lost none of their sparkle and none of their bouquet.

It is worth while asking ourselves why this should be—why these poems should "keep", apparently for ever, when the average modern poem turns sour overnight. And though all generalizations are dangerous I believe there is one which explains our problem, a very simple one . . . namely, that the eyes of the old ballad-singers were turned outwards, while the eyes of the modern lyric-writer are turned inwards.

The authors of the old ballads wrote when the world was young, and infinitely exciting, when nobody knew what mystery might not lie on the other side of the hill, when the moon was a golden lamp, lit by a personal God, when giants and monsters stalked, without the slightest doubt, in the valleys over the river. In such a world, what could a man do but stare about him, with bright eyes, searching the horizon, while his heart beat fast in the rhythm of a song?

But now—the mysteries have gone. We know, all too well, what lies on the other side of the hill. The scientists have long ago puffed out, scornfully, the golden lamp of the night . . . leaving us in the uttermost darkness. The giants and the monsters have either skulked away or have been tamed, and are engaged in writing their memoirs for the popular press. And so, in a world where everything is known (and nothing understood), the modern lyric-writer wearily averts his eyes, and stares into his own heart.

That way madness lies. All madmen are ferocious egotists, and so are all modern lyric-writers. That is the first and most vital difference between these ballads and their modern counterparts. The old ballad-singers hardly ever used the first person singular. The modern lyric-writer hardly ever uses anything else.

II

This is really such an important point that it is worth labouring.

Why is ballad-making a lost art? That it *is* a lost art there can be no question. Nobody who is painfully acquainted with the rambling, egotistical pieces of dreary versification, passing for modern "ballads", will deny it.

Ballad-making is a lost art for a very simple reason. Which is, that we are all, nowadays, too sicklied o'er with the pale cast of thought to receive emotions directly, without self-consciousness. If we are wounded, we are no longer able to sing a song about a clean sword, and a great cause, and a black enemy, and a waving flag. No—we must needs go into long descriptions of our pain, and abstruse calculations about its effect upon our souls.

It is not "we" who have changed. It is life that has changed. "We" are still men, with the same legs, arms and eyes as our ancestors. But life has so twisted things that there are no longer any clean swords nor great causes, nor black enemies. And the flags do not know which way to flutter, so contrary are the winds of the modern world. All is doubt. And doubt's colour is grey.

Grey is no colour for a ballad. Ballads are woven from stuff of primitive hue . . . the red blood gushing, the gold sun shining, the green grass growing, the white snow falling. Never will you find grey in a ballad. You will find the black of the night and the raven's wing, and the silver of a thousand stars. You will find the blue of many summer skies. But you will not find grey.

III

That is why ballad-making is a lost art. Or almost a lost art. For even in this odd and musty world of phantoms which we call the twentieth century, there are times when a man finds himself in a certain place at a certain hour and something happens to him which takes him out of himself. And a song is born, simply and sweetly, a song which other men can sing, for all time, and forget themselves.

Such a song was once written by a master at my old school, Marlborough. He was a Scot. But he loved Marlborough with the sort of love which the old ballad-mongers must have had-the sort of love which takes a man on wings, far from his foolish little body.

He wrote a song called "The Scotch Marlburian".

Here it is:—

Oh Marlborough, she's a toun o' touns
We will say that and mair,
We that ha' walked alang her douns
And snuffed her Wiltshire air.
A weary way ye'll hae to tramp
Afore ye match the green

O' Savernake and Barbery Camp
And a' that lies atween!

The infinite beauty of that phrase . . . "and a' that lies atween"! The infinite beauty as it is roared by seven hundred young throats in unison! For in that phrase there drifts a whole pageant of boyhood—the sound of cheers as a race is run on a stormy day in March, the tolling of the Chapel bell, the crack of ball against bat, the sighs of sleep in a long white dormitory.

But you may say "What is all this to me? I wasn't at Maryborough. I don't like schoolboys . . . they strike me as dirty, noisy, and usually foul-minded. Why should I go into raptures about such a song, which seems only to express a highly debatable approval of a certain method of education?"

If you are asking yourself that sort of question, you are obviously in very grave need of the tonic properties of this book. For after you have read it, you will wonder why you ever asked it.

IV

I go back and back to the same point, at the risk of boring you to distraction. For it is a point which has much more "to" it than the average modern will care to admit, unless he is forced to do so.

You remember the generalization about the eyes . . . how they used to look *out*, but now look *in*? Well, listen to this . . .

I'm feeling blue,
I don't know what to do,
'Cos *I* love you
And you don't love *me*.

The above masterpiece is, as far as I am aware, imaginary. But it represents a sort of *reductio ad absurdum* of thousands of lyrics which have been echoing over the post-war world. Nearly all these lyrics are melancholy, with the profound and primitive melancholy of the negro swamp, and they are all violently egotistical.

Now this, in the long run, is an influence of far greater evil than one would be inclined at first to admit. If countless young men, every night, are to clasp countless young women to their bosoms, and rotate over countless dancing-floors, muttering "I'm feeling blue . . . *I* don't know what to do", it is not unreasonable to suppose that they will subconsciously apply some of the lyric's mournful egotism to themselves.

Anybody who has even a nodding acquaintance with modern psychological science will be aware of the significance of "conditioning", as applied to the human temperament. The late M. Coue "conditioned" people into happiness by making them repeat, over and over again, the phrase "Every day in every way I grow better and better and better."

The modern lyric-monger exactly reverses M. Coue's doctrine. He makes the patient repeat "Every night, with all my might, I grow worse and worse and worse." Of course the "I" of the lyric-writer is an imaginary "I", but if any man sings *'I'm* feeling blue", often enough, to a catchy tune, he will be a superman if he does not eventually apply that "I" to himself.

But the "blueness" is really beside the point. It is the *egotism* of the modern ballad which is the trouble. Even when, as they occasionally do, the modern lyric-writers discover, to their astonishment, that they are feeling happy, they make the happiness such a personal issue that half its tonic value is destroyed. It is not, like the old ballads, just an outburst of delight, a sudden rapture at the warmth of the sun, or the song of the birds, or the glint of moonlight on a sword, or the dew in a woman's eyes. It is not an emotion so sweet and soaring that self is left behind, like a dull chrysalis, while the butterfly of the spirit flutters free. No . . . the chrysalis is never left behind, the "I", "I", "I", continues, in a maddening monotone. And we get this sort of thing . . .

> *I* want to be happy,
> But *I* can't be happy
> Till *I've* made you happy too.

And that, if you please, is one of the jolliest lyrics of the last decade! That was a song which made us all smile and set all our feet dancing!

Even when their tale was woven out of the stuff of tragedy, the old ballads were not tarnished with such morbid speculations. Read the tale of the beggar's daughter of Bethnal Green. One shudders to think what a modern lyric-writer would make of it. We should all be in tears before the end of the first chorus.

But here, a lovely girl leaves her blind father to search for fortune. She has many adventures, and in the end, she marries a knight. The ballad ends with words of almost childish simplicity, but they are words which ring with the true tone of happiness:—

> Thus was the feast ended with joye and delighte
> A bridegroome most happy then was the young knighte
> In joy and felicitie long lived hee
> All with his faire ladye, the pretty Bessee.

I said that the words were of almost childish simplicity. But the student of language, and the would-be writer, might do worse than study those words, if only to see how the cumulative effect of brightness and radiance is gained. You may think the words are artless, but just ponder, for a moment, the number of brilliant verbal symbols which are collected into that tiny verse. There are only four lines. But those lines contain these words . . .

Feast, joy, delight, bridegroom, happy, joy, young, felicity, fair, pretty.

18

Is that quite so artless, after all? Is it not rather like an old and primitive plaque, where colour is piled on colour till you would say the very wood will burst into flame . . . and yet, the total effect is one of happy simplicity?

V

How were the early ballads born? Who made them? One man or many? Were they written down, when they were still young, or was it only after the lapse of many generations, when their rhymes had been sharpened and their metres polished by constant repetition, that they were finally copied out?

To answer these questions would be one of the most fascinating tasks which the detective in letters could set himself. Grimm, listening in his fairyland, heard some of the earliest ballads, loved them, pondered on them, and suddenly startled the world by announcing that most ballads were not the work of a single author, but of the people at large. *Das Volk dichtet*, he said. And that phrase got him into a lot of trouble. People told him to get back to his fairyland and not make such ridiculous suggestions. For how, they asked, could a whole people make a poem? You might as well tell a thousand men to make a tune, limiting each of them to one note!

To invest Grimm's words with such an intention is quite unfair. [Footnote: For a discussion of Grimm's theories, together with much interesting speculation on the origin of the ballads, the reader should study the admirable introduction to *English and Scottish Popular Ballads*, published by George Harrap & Co., Ltd.] Obviously a multitude of people could not, deliberately, make a single poem any more than a multitude of people could, deliberately, make a single picture, one man doing the nose, one man an eye and so on. Such a suggestion is grotesque, and Grimm never meant it. If I might guess at what he meant, I would suggest that he was thinking that the origin of ballads must have been similar to the origin of the dance, (which was probably the earliest form of aesthetic expression known to man).

The dance was invented because it provided a means of prolonging ecstasy by art. It may have been an ecstasy of sex or an ecstasy of victory . . . that doesn't matter. The point is that it gave to a group of people an ordered means of expressing their delight instead of just leaping about and making loud cries, like the animals. And you may be sure that as the primitive dance began, there was always some member of the tribe a little more agile than the rest—some man who kicked a little higher or wriggled his body in an amusing way. And the rest of them copied him, and incorporated his step into their own.

Apply this analogy to the origin of ballads. It fits perfectly.

There has been a successful raid, or a wedding, or some great deed of daring, or some other phenomenal thing, natural or supernatural. And now that this day, which will ever linger in their memories, is drawing to its close, the members of the tribe draw round the fire and begin to make merry. The wine passes . . . and tongues are loosened. And someone says a phrase which has rhythm and a sparkle to it, and the phrase is caught up and goes round the fire, and is repeated from mouth to mouth. And then the local wit caps it with another phrase and a rhyme is born. For there is always a local wit in every community, however primitive. There is even a local wit in the monkey house at the zoo.

And once you have that single rhyme and that little piece of rhythm, you have the genesis of the whole thing. It may not be worked out that night, nor even by the men who first made it. The fire may long have died before the ballad is completed, and tall trees may stand over the men and women who were the first to tell the tale. But rhyme and rhythm are indestructible, if they are based on reality. "Not marble nor the gilded monuments of princes shall outlive this powerful rhyme."

And so it is that some of the loveliest poems in the language will ever remain anonymous. Needless to say, *all* the poems are not anonymous. As society became more civilized it was inevitable that the peculiar circumstances from which the earlier ballads sprang should become less frequent. Nevertheless, about nearly all of the ballads there is "a common touch", as though even the most self-conscious author had drunk deep of the well of tradition, that sparkling well in which so much beauty is distilled.

VI

But though the author or authors of most of the ballads may be lost in the lists of time, we know a good deal about the minstrels who sang them. And it is a happy thought that those minstrels were such considerable persons, so honourably treated, so generously esteemed. The modern mind, accustomed to think of the singer of popular songs either as a highly paid music-hall artist, at the top of the ladder, or a shivering street-singer, at the bottom of it, may find it difficult to conceive of a minstrel as a sort of ambassador of song, moving from court to court with dignity and ceremony.

Yet this was actually the case. In the ballad of King Estmere, for example, we see the minstrel finely mounted, and accompanied by a harpist, who sings his songs for him. This minstrel, too, moves among kings without any ceremony. As Percy has pointed out, "The further we carry our enquiries back, the greater respect we find paid to the professors of poetry and music among all the Celtic and Gothic nations. Their character was deemed so sacred that under its sanction our famous King Alfred made no scruple to enter the Danish camp, and was at once admitted to the king's headquarters."

And even so late as the time of Froissart, we have minstrels and heralds mentioned together, as those who might securely go into an enemy's country.

The reader will perhaps forgive me if I harp back, once more, to our present day and age, in view of the quite astonishing change in national psychology which that revelation implies. Minstrels and heralds were once allowed safe conduct into the enemy's country, in time of war. Yet, in the last war, it was considered right and proper to hiss the work of Beethoven off the stage, and responsible newspapers seriously suggested that never again should a note of German music, of however great antiquity, be heard in England! We are supposed to have progressed towards internationalism, nowadays. Whereas, in reality, we have grown more and more frenziedly national. We are very far behind the age of Froissart, when there was a true internationalism—the internationalism of art.

To some of us that is still a very real internationalism. When we hear a Beethoven sonata we do not think of it as issuing from the brain of a "Teuton" but as blowing from the eternal heights of music whose winds list nothing of frontiers.

Man *needs* song, for he is a singing animal. Moreover, he needs communal song, for he is a social animal. The military authorities realized this very cleverly, and they encouraged the troops, during the war, to sing on every possible occasion. Crazy pacifists, like myself, may find it almost unbearably bitter to think that on each side of various frontiers young men were being trained to sing themselves to death, in a struggle which was hideously impersonal, a struggle of machinery, in which the only winners were the armament manufacturers. And crazy pacifists might draw a very sharp line indeed between the songs which celebrated real personal struggles in the tiny wars of the past, and the songs which were merely the prelude to thousands of puzzled young men suddenly finding themselves choking in chlorine gas, in the wars of the present.

But even the craziest pacifist could not fail to be moved by some of the ballads of the last war. To me, "Tipperary" is still the most moving tune in the world. It happens to be a very good tune, from the musician's point of view, a tune that Handel would not have been ashamed to write, but that is not the point. Its emotional qualities are due to its associations. Perhaps that is how it has always been, with ballads. From the standard of pure aesthetics, one ought not to consider "associations" in judging a poem or a tune, but with a song like "Tipperary" you would be an inhuman prig if you didn't. We all have our "associations" with this particular tune. For me, it recalls a window in Hampstead, on a grey day in October 1914. I had been having the measles, and had not been allowed to go back to school. Then suddenly, down the street, that tune echoed. And they came marching, and marching, and marching. And they were all so happy.

So happy.

VII

"Tipperary" is a true ballad, which is why it is included in this book. So is "John Brown's Body". They were not written as ballads but they have been promoted to that proud position by popular vote.

It will now be clear, from the foregoing remarks, that there are thousands of poems, labelled "ballads" from the eighteenth century, through the romantic movement, and onwards, which are not ballads at all. Swinburne's ballads, which so shocked our grandparents, bore about as much relation to the true ballads as a vase of wax fruit to a hawker's barrow. They were lovely patterns of words, woven like some exquisite, foaming lace, but they were Swinburne, Swinburne all the time. They had nothing to do with the common people. The common people would not have understood a word of them.

Ballads *must* be popular. And that is why it will always remain one of the weirdest paradoxes of literature that the only man, except Kipling, who has written a true ballad in the last fifty years is the man who despised the people, who shrank from them, and jeered at them, from his little gilded niche in Piccadilly. I refer, of course, to Oscar Wilde's "Ballad of Reading Gaol." It was a true ballad, and it was the best thing he ever wrote. For it was written *de profundis*, when his hands were bloody with labour and his tortured spirit had been down to the level of the lowest, to the level of the pavement . . . nay, lower . . . to the gutter itself. And in the gutter, with agony, he learned the meaning of song.

Ballads begin and end with the people. You cannot escape that fact. And therefore, if I wished to collect the ballads of the future, the songs which will endure into the next century (if there *is* any song in the next century), I should not rake through the contemporary poets, in the hope of finding gems of lasting brilliance. No. I should go to the music-halls. I should listen to the sort of thing they sing when the faded lady with the high bust steps forward and shouts, "Now then, boys, all together!"

Unless you can write the words "Now then, boys, all together", at the top of a ballad, it is not really a ballad at all. That may sound a sweeping statement, but it is true.

In the present-day music-halls, although they have fallen from their high estate, we should find a number of these songs which seem destined for immortality. One of these is "Don't 'ave any more, Mrs. Moore."

Do you remember it?

> Don't 'ave any more, Mrs. Moore!
> Mrs. Moore, oh don't 'ave any more!
> Too many double gins
> Give the ladies double chins,
> So don't 'ave any more, Mrs. Moore!

The whole of English "low life" (which is much the most exciting part of English life) is in that lyric. It is as vivid as a Rowlandson cartoon. How well we know Mrs. Moore! How plainly we see her . . . the amiable, coarse-mouthed, generous-hearted tippler, with her elbow on countless counters, her damp coppers clutched in her rough hands, her eyes staring, a little vacantly, about her. Some may think it is a sordid picture, but I am sure that they cannot know Mrs. Moore very well if they think that. They cannot know her bitter struggles, her silent heroisms, nor her sardonic humour.

Lyrics such as these will, I believe, endure long after many of the most renowned and fashionable poets of to-day are forgotten. They all have the same quality, that they can be prefaced by that inspiring sentence, "Now then, boys—all together!" Or to put it another way, as in the ballad of George Barnwell,

> All youths of fair England
> That dwell both far and near,
> Regard my story that I tell
> And to my song give ear.

That may sound more dignified, but it amounts to the same thing!

VIII

But if the generation to come will learn a great deal from the few popular ballads which we are still creating in our music-halls, how much more shall we learn of history from these ballads, which rang through the whole country, and were impregnated with the spirit of a whole people! These ballads *are* history, and as such they should be recognised.

It has always seemed to me that we teach history in the wrong way. We give boys the impression that it is an affair only of kings and queens and great statesmen, of generals and admirals, and such-like bores. Thousands of boys could probably draw you a map of many pettifogging little campaigns, with startling accuracy, but not one in a thousand could tell you what the private soldier carried in his knapsack. You could get sheaves of competent essays, from any school, dealing with such things as the Elizabethan ecclesiastical settlement, but how many boys could tell you, even vaguely, what an English home was like, what they ate, what coins were used, how their rooms were lit, and what they paid their servants?

In other words, how many history masters ever take the trouble to sketch in the great background, the life of the common people? How many even realize their *existence*, except on occasions of national disaster, such as the Black Plague?

A proper study of the ballads would go a long way towards remedying this defect. Thomas Percy, whose *Reliques* must ever be the main source of our information on all questions connected with ballads, has pointed out that all the great events of the country have, sooner or later, found their way into the country's song-book. But it is not only the resounding names that are celebrated. In the ballads we hear the echoes of the street, the rude laughter and the pointed jests. Sometimes these ring so plainly that they need no explanation. At other times, we have to go to Percy or to some of his successors to realize the true significance of the song.

For example, the famous ballad "John Anderson my Jo" seems, at first sight, to be innocent of any polemical intention. But it was written during the Reformation when, as Percy dryly observes, "the Muses were deeply engaged in religious controversy." The zeal of the Scottish reformers was at its height, and this zeal found vent in many a pasquil discharged at Popery. It caused them, indeed, in their frenzy, to compose songs which were grossly licentious, and to sing these songs in rasping voices to the tunes of some of the most popular hymns in the Latin Service.

"John Anderson my Jo" was such a ballad composed for such an occasion. And Percy, who was more qualified than any other man to read between the lines, has pointed out that the first stanza contains a satirical allusion to the luxury of the popish clergy, while the second, which makes an apparently light reference to "seven bairns", is actually concerned with the seven sacraments, five of which were the spurious offspring of Mother Church.

Thus it was in a thousand cases. The ballads, even the lightest and most blossoming of them, were deep-rooted in the soil of English history. How different from anything that we possess to-day! Great causes do not lead men to song, nowadays they lead them to write letters to the newspapers. A national thanksgiving cannot call forth a single rhyme or a single bar of music. Who can remember a solitary verse of thanksgiving, from any of our poets, in commemoration of any of the victories of the Great War? Who can recall even a fragment of verse in praise of the long-deferred coming of Peace?

Very deeply significant is it that our only method of commemorating Armistice Day was by a two minutes silence. No song. No music. Nothing. The best thing we could do, we felt, was to keep quiet.

MANDALAY

Mandalay

By the old Moulmein Pagoda, lookin' eastward to the sea,
There's a Burma girl a-settin', and I know she thinks o' me;
For the wind is in the palm-trees, and the temple-bells they say:
'Come you back, you British soldier; come you back to Mandalay!'
Come you back to Mandalay,
Where the old Flotilla lay:
Can't you 'ear their paddles chunkin' from Rangoon to Mandalay?
On the road to Mandalay,
Where the flyin'-fishes play,
An' the dawn comes up like thunder outer China 'crost the Bay!

'Er petticoat was yaller an' 'er little cap was green,
An' 'er name was Supi-yaw-lat—jes' the same as Theebaw's Queen,
An' I seed her first a-smokin' of a whackin' white cheroot,
An' a-wastin' Christian kisses on an 'eathen idol's foot:
    Bloomin' idol made o' mud—

Wot they called the Great Gawd Budd—
Plucky lot she cared for idols when I kissed 'er where she stud!
On the road to Mandalay . . .

When the mist was on the rice-fields an' the sun was droppin' slow,
She'd git 'er little banjo an' she'd sing *'Kulla-lo-lo!'*
With 'er arm upon my shoulder an' 'er cheek agin my cheek
We useter watch the steamers an' the *hathis* pilin' teak.
    Elephints a-pilin' teak
    In the sludgy, squdgy creek,
    Where the silence 'ung that 'eavy you was 'arf afraid to speak!
    On the road to Mandalay . . .

But that's all shove be'ind me—long ago an' fur away,
An' there ain't no 'busses runnin' from the Bank to Mandalay;
An' I'm learnin' 'ere in London what the ten-year soldier tells:
'If you've 'eard the East a-callin', you won't never 'eed naught else.'
    No! you won't 'eed nothin' else
    But them spicy garlic smells,
    An' the sunshine an' the palm-trees an' the tinkly temple-bells;
    On the road to Mandalay . . .

I am sick o' wastin' leather on these gritty pavin'-stones,
An' the blasted Henglish drizzle wakes the fever in my bones;
Tho' I walks with fifty 'ousemaids outer Chelsea to the Strand,
An' they talks a lot o' lovin', but wot do they understand?
    Beefy face an' grubby 'and—
    Law! wot do they understand?
    I've a neater, sweeter maiden in a cleaner, greener land!
    On the road to Mandalay . . .

Ship me somewheres east of Suez, where the best is like the worst,
Where there aren't no Ten Commandments an' a man can raise a thirst;
For the temple-bells are callin', an' it's there that I would be—
By the old Moulmein Pagoda, looking lazy at the sea;
    On the road to Mandalay,
    Where the old Flotilla lay,
    With our sick beneath the awnings when we went to Mandalay!
    O the road to Mandalay,
    Where the flyin'-fishes play,
    An' the dawn comes up like thunder outer China 'crost the Bay!

THE FROLICKSOME DUKE

or
THE TINKER'S GOOD FORTUNE

Now as fame does report a young duke keeps a court,
One that pleases his fancy with frolicksome sport:
But amongst all the rest, here is one I protest,
Which will make you to smile when you hear the true jest:
A poor tinker he found, lying drunk on the ground,
As secure in a sleep as if laid in a swound.

The Duke said to his men, William, Richard, and Ben,
Take him home to my palace, we'll sport with him then.
O'er a horse he was laid, and with care soon convey'd
To the palace, altho' he was poorly arrai'd:

Then they stript off his cloaths, both his shirt, shoes and hose,
And they put him to bed for to take his repose.

Having pull'd off his shirt, which was all over durt,
They did give him clean holland, this was no great hurt:
On a bed of soft down, like a lord of renown,
They did lay him to sleep the drink out of his crown.
In the morning when day, then admiring he lay,
For to see the rich chamber both gaudy and gay.

Now he lay something late, in his rich bed of state,
Till at last knights and squires they on him did wait;
And the chamberling bare, then did likewise declare,
He desired to know what apparel he'd ware:
The poor tinker amaz'd on the gentleman gaz'd,
And admired how he to this honour was rais'd.

Tho' he seem'd something mute, yet he chose a rich suit,
Which he straitways put on without longer dispute;
With a star on his side, which the tinker offt ey'd,
And it seem'd for to swell him "no" little with pride;
For he said to himself, Where is Joan my sweet wife?
Sure she never did see me so fine in her life.

From a convenient place, the right duke his good grace
Did observe his behaviour in every case.
To a garden of state, on the tinker they wait,
Trumpets sounding before him: thought he, this is great:
Where an hour or two, pleasant walks he did view,
With commanders and squires in scarlet and blew.

A fine dinner was drest, both for him and his guests,
He was plac'd at the table above all the rest,
In a rich chair "or bed," lin'd with fine crimson red,
With a rich golden canopy over his head:
As he sat at his meat, the musick play'd sweet,
With the choicest of singing his joys to compleat.

While the tinker did dine, he had plenty of wine,
Rich canary with sherry and tent superfine.
Like a right honest soul, faith, he took off his bowl,
Till at last he began for to tumble and roul
From his chair to the floor, where he sleeping did snore,
Being seven times drunker than ever before.

Then the duke did ordain, they should strip him amain,
And restore him his old leather garments again:
'T was a point next the worst, yet perform it they must,
And they carry'd him strait, where they found him at first;
There he slept all the night, as indeed well he might;
But when he did waken, his joys took their flight.

For his glory "to him" so pleasant did seem,
That he thought it to be but a meer golden dream;
Till at length he was brought to the duke, where he sought
For a pardon, as fearing he had set him at nought;
But his highness he said, Thou 'rt a jolly bold blade,
Such a frolick before I think never was plaid.

Then his highness bespoke him a new suit and cloak,
Which he gave for the sake of this frolicksome joak;
Nay, and five-hundred pound, with ten acres of ground,
Thou shalt never, said he, range the counteries round,

Crying old brass to mend, for I'll be thy good friend,
Nay, and Joan thy sweet wife shall my duchess attend.

Then the tinker reply'd, What! must Joan my sweet bride
Be a lady in chariots of pleasure to ride?
Must we have gold and land ev'ry day at command?
Then I shall be a squire I well understand:
Well I thank your good grace, and your love I embrace,
I was never before in so happy a case.

THE KNIGHT & SHEPHERD'S DAUGHTER

There was a shepherd's daughter
 Came tripping on the waye;
And there by chance a knighte shee mett,
 Which caused her to staye.

Good morrowe to you, beauteous maide,
 These words pronounced hee:
O I shall dye this daye, he sayd,
 If Ive not my wille of thee.

The Lord forbid, the maide replyde,
 That you shold waxe so wode!
"But for all that shee could do or saye,
 He wold not be withstood."

Sith you have had your wille of mee,
 And put me to open shame,

Now, if you are a courteous knighte,
    Tell me what is your name?

Some do call mee Jacke, sweet heart,
    And some do call mee Jille;
But when I come to the kings faire courte
    They call me Wilfulle Wille.

He sett his foot into the stirrup,
    And awaye then he did ride;
She tuckt her girdle about her middle,
    And ranne close by his side.

But when she came to the brode water,
    She sett her brest and swamme;
And when she was got out againe,
    She tooke to her heels and ranne.

He never was the courteous knighte,
    To saye, faire maide, will ye ride?
"And she was ever too loving a maide
    To saye, sir knighte abide."

When she came to the kings faire courte,
    She knocked at the ring;
So readye was the king himself
    To let this faire maide in.

Now Christ you save, my gracious liege,
    Now Christ you save and see,
You have a knighte within your courte,
    This daye hath robbed mee.

What hath he robbed thee of, sweet heart?
　　Of purple or of pall?
Or hath he took thy gaye gold ring
　　From off thy finger small?

He hath not robbed mee, my liege,
　　Of purple nor of pall:
But he hath gotten my maiden head,
　　Which grieves mee worst of all.

Now if he be a batchelor,
　　His bodye He give to thee;
But if he be a married man,
　　High hanged he shall bee.

He called downe his merrye men all,
　　By one, by two, by three;
Sir William used to bee the first,
　　But nowe the last came hee.

He brought her downe full fortye pounde,
　　Tyed up withinne a glove:
Faire maide, He give the same to thee;
　　Go, seeke thee another love.

O Ile have none of your gold, she sayde,
　　Nor Ile have none of your fee;
But your faire bodye I must have,
　　The king hath granted mee.

Sir William ranne and fetched her then
　　Five hundred pound in golde,

Saying, faire maide, take this to thee,
  Thy fault will never be tolde.

Tis not the gold that shall mee tempt,
  These words then answered shee,
But your own bodye I must have,
  The king hath granted mee.

Would I had dranke the water cleare,
  When I did drinke the wine,
Rather than any shepherds brat
  Shold bee a ladye of mine!

Would I had drank the puddle foule,
  When I did drink the ale,
Rather than ever a shepherds brat
  Shold tell me such a tale!

A shepherds brat even as I was,
  You mote have let me bee,
I never had come to the kings faire courte,
  To crave any love of thee.

He sett her on a milk-white steede,
  And himself upon a graye;
He hung a bugle about his necke,
  And soe they rode awaye.

But when they came unto the place,
  Where marriage-rites were done,
She proved herself a dukes daughter,
  And he but a squires sonne.

Now marrye me, or not, sir knight,
   Your pleasure shall be free:
If you make me ladye of one good towne,
   He make you lord of three.

Ah! cursed bee the gold, he sayd,
   If thou hadst not been trewe,
I shold have forsaken my sweet love,
   And have changed her for a newe.

And now their hearts being linked fast,
   They joyned hand in hande:
Thus he had both purse, and person too,
   And all at his commande.

KING ESTMERE

Hearken to me, gentlemen,
    Come and you shall heare;
Ile tell you of two of the boldest brethren
    That ever borne y-were.

The tone of them was Adler younge,
   The tother was kyng Estmere;
The were as bolde men in their deeds,
   As any were farr and neare.

As they were drinking ale and wine
   Within kyng Estmeres halle:
When will ye marry a wyfe, brother,
   A wyfe to glad us all?

Then bespake him kyng Estmere,
   And answered him hastilee:
I know not that ladye in any land
   That's able to marrye with mee.

Kyng Adland hath a daughter, brother,
   Men call her bright and sheene;
If I were kyng here in your stead,
   That ladye shold be my queene.

Saies, Reade me, reade me, deare brother,
   Throughout merry England,
Where we might find a messenger
   Betwixt us towe to sende.

Saies, You shal ryde yourselfe, brother,
   Ile beare you companye;
Many throughe fals messengers are deceived,
   And I feare lest soe shold wee.

Thus the renisht them to ryde
   Of twoe good renisht steeds,

And when the came to kyng Adlands halle,
   Of redd gold shone their weeds.

And when the came to kyng Adlands hall
   Before the goodlye gate,
There they found good kyng Adland
   Rearing himselfe theratt.

Now Christ thee save, good kyng Adland;
   Now Christ you save and see.
Sayd, You be welcome, kyng Estmere,
   Right hartilye to mee.

You have a daughter, said Adler younge,
   Men call her bright and sheene,
My brother wold marrye her to his wiffe,
   Of Englande to be queene.

Yesterday was att my deere daughter
   Syr Bremor the kyng of Spayne;
And then she nicked him of naye,
   And I doubt sheele do you the same.

The kyng of Spayne is a foule paynim,
   And 'leeveth on Mahound;
And pitye it were that fayre ladye
   Shold marrye a heathen hound.

But grant to me, sayes kyng Estmere,
   For my love I you praye;
That I may see your daughter deere
   Before I goe hence awaye.

Although itt is seven yeers and more
    Since my daughter was in halle,
She shall come once downe for your sake
    To glad my guestes alle.

Downe then came that mayden fayre,
    With ladyes laced in pall,
And halfe a hundred of bold knightes,
    To bring her from bowre to hall;
And as many gentle squiers,
    To tend upon them all.

The talents of golde were on her head sette,
    Hanged low downe to her knee;
And everye ring on her small finger
    Shone of the chrystall free.

Saies, God you save, my deere madam;
    Saies, God you save and see.
Said, You be welcome, kyng Estmere,
    Right welcome unto mee.

And if you love me, as you saye,
    Soe well and hartilye,
All that ever you are comin about
    Sooner sped now itt shal bee.

Then bespake her father deare:
    My daughter, I saye naye;
Remember well the kyng of Spayne,
    What he sayd yesterday.

He wold pull downe my hales and castles,
    And reeve me of my life.
I cannot blame him if he doe,
    If I reave him of his wyfe.

Your castles and your towres, father,
    Are stronglye built aboute;
And therefore of the king of Spaine
    Wee neede not stande in doubt.

Plight me your troth, nowe, kyng Estmere,
    By heaven and your righte hand,
That you will marrye me to your wyfe,
    And make me queene of your land.

Then kyng Estmere he plight his troth
    By heaven and his righte hand,
That he wolde marrye her to his wyfe,
    And make her queene of his land.

And he tooke leave of that ladye fayre,
    To goe to his owne countree,
To fetche him dukes and lordes and knightes,
    That marryed the might bee.

They had not ridden scant a myle,
    A myle forthe of the towne,
But in did come the kyng of Spayne,
    With kempes many one.

But in did come the kyng of Spayne,
    With manye a bold barone,

Tone day to marrye kyng Adlands daughter,
  Tother daye to carrye her home.

Shee sent one after kyng Estmere
  In all the spede might bee,
That he must either turne againe and fighte,
  Or goe home and loose his ladye.

One whyle then the page he went,
  Another while he ranne;
Tull he had oretaken king Estmere,
    I wis, he never blanne.

Tydings, tydings, kyng Estmere!
  What tydinges nowe, my boye?
O tydinges I can tell to you,
  That will you sore annoye.

You had not ridden scant a mile,
  A mile out of the towne,
But in did come the kyng of Spayne
  With kempes many a one:

But in did come the kyng of Spayne
  With manye a bold barone,
Tone daye to marrye king Adlands daughter,
  Tother daye to carry her home.

My ladye fayre she greetes you well,
  And ever-more well by mee:
You must either turne againe and fighte,
  Or goe home and loose your ladye.

Saies, Reade me, reade me, deere brother,
    My reade shall ryde at thee,
Whether it is better to turne and fighte,
    Or goe home and loose my ladye.

Now hearken to me, sayes Adler yonge,
    And your reade must rise at me,
I quicklye will devise a waye
    To sette thy ladye free.

My mother was a westerne woman,
    And learned in gramarye,
And when I learned at the schole,
    Something she taught itt mee.

There growes an hearbe within this field,
    And iff it were but knowne,
His color, which is whyte and redd,
    It will make blacke and browne:

His color, which is browne and blacke,
    Itt will make redd and whyte;
That sworde is not in all Englande,
    Upon his coate will byte.

And you shall be a harper, brother,
    Out of the north countrye;
And He be your boy, soe faine of fighte,
    And beare your harpe by your knee.

And you shal be the best harper,
    That ever tooke harpe in hand;

And I wil be the best singer,
    That ever sung in this lande.

Itt shal be written on our forheads
    All and in grammarye,
That we towe are the boldest men,
    That are in all Christentye.

And thus they renisht them to ryde,
    On tow good renish steedes;
And when they came to king Adlands hall,
    Of redd gold shone their weedes.

And whan they came to kyng Adlands hall,
    Untill the fayre hall yate,
There they found a proud porter
    Rearing himselfe thereatt.

Sayes, Christ thee save, thou proud porter;
    Sayes, Christ thee save and see.
Nowe you be welcome, sayd the porter,
    Of whatsoever land ye bee.

Wee beene harpers, sayd Adler younge,
    Come out of the northe countrye;
Wee beene come hither untill this place,
    This proud weddinge for to see.

Sayd, And your color were white and redd,
    As it is blacke and browne,
I wold saye king Estmere and his brother,
    Were comen untill this towne.

Then they pulled out a ryng of gold,
    Layd itt on the porters arme:
And ever we will thee, proud porter,
    Thow wilt saye us no harme.

Sore he looked on king Estmere,
    And sore he handled the ryng,
Then opened to them the fayre hall yates,
    He lett for no kind of thyng.

King Estmere he stabled his steede
    Soe fayre att the hall bord;
The froth, that came from his brydle bitte,
    Light in kyng Bremors beard.

Saies, Stable thy steed, thou proud harper,
    Saies, Stable him in the stalle;
It doth not beseeme a proud harper
    To stable 'him' in a kyngs halle.

My ladde he is no lither, he said,
    He will doe nought that's meete;
And is there any man in this hall
    Were able him to beate

Thou speakst proud words, sayes the king of Spaine,
    Thou harper, here to mee:
There is a man within this halle
    Will beate thy ladd and thee.

O let that man come downe, he said,
    A sight of him wold I see;

And when hee hath beaten well my ladd,
   Then he shall beate of mee.

Downe then came the kemperye man,
   And looketh him in the eare;
For all the gold, that was under heaven,
   He durst not neigh him neare.

And how nowe, kempe, said the Kyng of Spaine,
   And how what aileth thee?
He saies, It is writt in his forhead
   All and in gramarye,
That for all the gold that is under heaven
   I dare not neigh him nye.

Then Kyng Estmere pulld forth his harpe,
   And plaid a pretty thinge:
The ladye upstart from the borde,
   And wold have gone from the king.

Stay thy harpe, thou proud harper,
   For Gods love I pray thee,
For and thou playes as thou beginns,
   Thou'lt till my bryde from mee.

He stroake upon his harpe againe,
   And playd a pretty thinge;
The ladye lough a loud laughter,
   As shee sate by the king.

Saies, Sell me thy harpe, thou proud harper,
   And thy stringes all,

For as many gold nobles 'thou shall have'
   As heere bee ringes in the hall.

What wold ye doe with my harpe,' he sayd,'
   If I did sell itt yee?
"To playe my wiffe and me a fitt,
   When abed together wee bee."

Now sell me, quoth hee, thy bryde soe gay,
   As shee sitts by thy knee,
And as many gold nobles I will give,
   As leaves been on a tree.

And what wold ye doe with my bryde soe gay,
   Iff I did sell her thee?
More seemelye it is for her fayre bodye
   To lye by mee then thee.

Hee played agayne both loud and shrille,
   And Adler he did syng,
"O ladye, this is thy owne true love;
   Noe harper, but a kyng.

"O ladye, this is thy owne true love,
   As playnlye thou mayest see;
And He rid thee of that foule paynim,
   Who partes thy love and thee."

The ladye looked, the ladye blushte,
   And blushte and lookt agayne,
While Adler he hath drawne his brande,
   And hath the Sowdan slayne.

Up then rose the kemperye men,
    And loud they gan to crye:
Ah; traytors, yee have slayne our kyng,
    And therefore yee shall dye.

Kyng Estmere threwe the harpe asyde,
    And swith he drew his brand;
And Estmere he, and Adler yonge
    Right stiffe in slodr can stand.

And aye their swordes soe sore can byte,
    Throughe help of Gramarye,
That soone they have slayne the kempery men,
    Or forst them forth to flee.

Kyng Estmere took that fayre ladye,
    And marryed her to his wiffe,
And brought her home to merry England
    With her to leade his life.

KING JOHN AND
THE ABBOT OF CANTERBURY

An ancient story Ile tell you anon
Of a notable prince, that was called King John;
And he ruled England with maine and with might,
For he did great wrong, and maintein'd little right.

And Ile tell you a story, a story so merrye,
Concerning the Abbot of Canterburye;
How for his house-keeping, and high renowne,
They rode poste for him to fair London towne.

An hundred men, the king did heare say,
The abbot kept in his house every day;
And fifty golde chaynes, without any doubt,
In velvet coates waited the abbot about.

How now, father abbot, I heare it of thee,
Thou keepest a farre better house than mee,
And for thy house-keeping and high renowne,
I feare thou work'st treason against my crown.

My liege, quo' the abbot, I would it were knowne,
I never spend nothing, but what is my owne;
And I trust, your grace will doe me no deere,
For spending of my owne true-gotten geere.

Yes, yes, father abbot, thy fault it is highe,
And now for the same thou needest must dye;
For except thou canst answer me questions three,
Thy head shall be smitten from thy bodie.

And first, quo' the king, when I'm in this stead,
With my crowne of golde so faire on my head,
Among all my liege-men so noble of birthe,
Thou must tell me to one penny what I am worthe.

Secondlye, tell me, without any doubt,
How soone I may ride the whole world about.
And at the third question thou must not shrink,
But tell me here truly what I do think.

O, these are hard questions for my shallow witt,
Nor I cannot answer your grace as yet:
But if you will give me but three weekes space,
Ile do my endeavour to answer your grace.

Now three weeks space to thee will I give,
And that is the longest time thou hast to live;

For if thou dost not answer my questions three,
Thy lands and thy livings are forfeit to mee.

Away rode the abbot all sad at that word,
And he rode to Cambridge, and Oxenford;
But never a doctor there was so wise,
That could with his learning an answer devise.

Then home rode the abbot of comfort so cold,
And he mett his shepheard a going to fold:
How now, my lord abbot, you are welcome home;
What newes do you bring us from good King John?

"Sad newes, sad newes, shepheard, I must give;
That I have but three days more to live:
For if I do not answer him questions three,
My head will be smitten from my bodie.

The first is to tell him there in that stead,
With his crowne of golde so fair on his head,
Among all his liege men so noble of birth,
To within one penny of all what he is worth.

The seconde, to tell him, without any doubt,
How soon he may ride this whole world about:
And at the third question I must not shrinke,
But tell him there truly what he does thinke."

Now cheare up, sire abbot, did you never hear yet,
That a fool he may learn a wise man witt?
Lend me horse, and serving men, and your apparel,
And I'll ride to London to answere your quarrel.

Nay frowne not, if it hath bin told unto mee,
I am like your lordship, as ever may bee:
And if you will but lend me your gowne,
There is none shall knowe us at fair London towne.

Now horses, and serving-men thou shalt have,
With sumptuous array most gallant and brave;
With crozier, and miter, and rochet, and cope,
Fit to appeare 'fore our fader the pope.

Now welcome, sire abbott, the king he did say,
'Tis well thou'rt come back to keep thy day;
For and if thou canst answer my questions three,
Thy life and thy living both saved shall bee.

And first, when thou seest me here in this stead,
With my crowne of gold so fair on my head,
Among all my liege-men so noble of birthe,
Tell me to one penny what I am worth.

"For thirty pence our Saviour was sold
Amonge the false Jewes, as I have bin told;
And twenty nine is the worth of thee,
For I thinke, thou art one penny worser than hee."

The king he laughed, and swore by St. Bittel,
I did not thinke I had been worth so littel!
—Now secondly tell me, without any doubt,
How soon I may ride this whole world about.

"You must rise with the sun, and ride with the same,
Until the next morning he riseth againe;

And then your grace need not make any doubt,
But in twenty-four hours you'll ride it about."

The king he laughed, and swore by St. Jone,
I did not think, it could be gone so soone!
—Now from the third question thou must not shrinke,
But tell me here truly what I do thinke.

"Yea, that shall I do, and make your grace merry:
You thinke I'm the Abbot of Canterbury;
But I'm his poor shepheard, as plain you may see,
That am come to beg pardon for him and for mee."

The king he laughed, and swore by the masse,
He make thee lord abbot this day in his place!
"Now naye, my liege, be not in such speede,
For alacke I can neither write ne reade."

Four nobles a weeke, then I will give thee,
For this merry jest thou hast showne unto mee;
And tell the old abbot, when thou comest home,
Thou hast brought him a pardon from good King John.

BARBARA ALLEN'S CRUELTY

Barbara Allen's Cruelty

In Scarlet towne where I was borne,
   There was a faire maid dwellin,
Made every youth crye, Wel-awaye!
   Her name was Barbara Allen.

All in the merrye month of May,
    When greene buds they were swellin,
Yong Jemmye Grove on his death-bed lay,
    For love of Barbara Allen.

He sent his man unto her then,
    To the town where shee was dwellin;
You must come to my master deare,
    Giff your name be Barbara Alien.

For death is printed on his face,
    And ore his harte is stealin:
Then haste away to comfort him,
    O lovelye Barbara Alien.

Though death be printed on his face,
    And ore his harte is stealin,
Yet little better shall he bee
    For bonny Barbara Alien.

So slowly, slowly, she came up,
    And slowly she came nye him;
And all she sayd, when there she came,
    Yong man, I think y'are dying.

He turned his face unto her strait,
    With deadlye sorrow sighing;
O lovely maid, come pity mee,
    Ime on my death-bed lying.

If on your death-bed you doe lye,
    What needs the tale you are tellin;

I cannot keep you from your death;
  Farewell, sayd Barbara Alien.

He turned his face unto the wall,
  As deadlye pangs he fell in:
Adieu! adieu! adieu to you all,
  Adieu to Barbara Allen.

As she was walking ore the fields,
  She heard the bell a knellin;
And every stroke did seem to saye,
  Unworthye Barbara Allen.

She turned her bodye round about,
  And spied the corps a coming:
Laye down, lay down the corps, she sayd,
  That I may look upon him.

With scornful eye she looked downe,
  Her cheeke with laughter swellin;
Whilst all her friends cryd out amaine,
  Unworthye Barbara Allen.

When he was dead, and laid in grave,
  Her harte was struck with sorrowe,
O mother, mother, make my bed,
  For I shall dye to-morrowe.

Hard-harted creature him to slight,
  Who loved me so dearlye:
O that I had beene more kind to him
  When he was alive and neare me!

She, on her death-bed as she laye,
　　Beg'd to be buried by him;
And sore repented of the daye,
　　That she did ere denye him.

Farewell, she sayd, ye virgins all,
　　And shun the fault I fell in:
Henceforth take warning by the fall
　　Of cruel Barbara Allen.

FAIR ROSAMOND

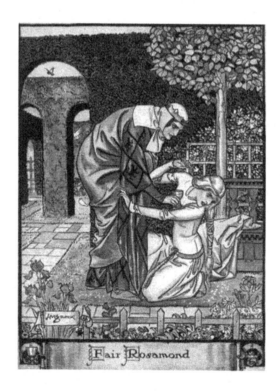

Fair Rosamond

When as King Henry rulde this land,
   The second of that name,
Besides the queene, he dearly lovde
   A faire and comely dame.

Most peerlesse was her beautye founde,
    Her favour, and her face;
A sweeter creature in this worlde
    Could never prince embrace.

Her crisped lockes like threads of golde
    Appeard to each mans sight;
Her sparkling eyes, like Orient pearles,
    Did cast a heavenlye light.

The blood within her crystal cheekes
    Did such a colour drive,
As though the lillye and the rose
    For mastership did strive.

Yea Rosamonde, fair Rosamonde,
    Her name was called so,
To whom our queene, dame Ellinor,
    Was known a deadlye foe.

The king therefore, for her defence,
    Against the furious queene,
At Woodstocke builded such a bower,
    The like was never scene.

Most curiously that bower was built
    Of stone and timber strong,
An hundred and fifty doors
    Did to this bower belong:

And they so cunninglye contriv'd
    With turnings round about,

That none but with a clue of thread,
    Could enter in or out.

And for his love and ladyes sake,
    That was so faire and brighte,
The keeping of this bower he gave
    Unto a valiant knighte.

But fortune, that doth often frowne
    Where she before did smile,
The kinges delighte and ladyes so
    Full soon shee did beguile:

For why, the kinges ungracious sonne,
    Whom he did high advance,
Against his father raised warres
    Within the realme of France.

But yet before our comelye king
    The English land forsooke,
Of Rosamond, his lady faire,
    His farewelle thus he tooke:

"My Rosamonde, my only Rose,
    That pleasest best mine eye:
The fairest flower in all the worlde
    To feed my fantasye:

The flower of mine affected heart,
    Whose sweetness doth excelle:
My royal Rose, a thousand times
    I bid thee nowe farwelle!

For I must leave my fairest flower,
  My sweetest Rose, a space,
And cross the seas to famous France,
  Proud rebelles to abase.

But yet, my Rose, be sure thou shalt
  My coming shortlye see,
And in my heart, when hence I am,
  Ile beare my Rose with mee."

When Rosamond, that ladye brighte,
  Did heare the king saye soe,
The sorrowe of her grieved heart
  Her outward lookes did showe;

And from her cleare and crystall eyes
  The teares gusht out apace,
Which like the silver-pearled dewe
  Ranne downe her comely face.

Her lippes, erst like the corall redde,
  Did waxe both wan and pale,
And for the sorrow she conceivde
  Her vitall spirits faile;

And falling down all in a swoone
  Before King Henryes face,
Full oft he in his princelye armes
  Her bodye did embrace:

And twentye times, with watery eyes,
  He kist her tender cheeke,

Untill he had revivde againe
   Her senses milde and meeke.

Why grieves my Rose, my sweetest Rose?
   The king did often say.
Because, quoth shee, to bloodye warres
   My lord must part awaye.

But since your grace on forrayne coastes
   Amonge your foes unkinde
Must goe to hazard life and limbe,
   Why should I staye behinde?

Nay rather, let me, like a page,
   Your sworde and target beare;
That on my breast the blowes may lighte,
   Which would offend you there.

Or lett mee, in your royal tent,
   Prepare your bed at nighte,
And with sweete baths refresh your grace,
   Ar your returne from fighte.

So I your presence may enjoye
   No toil I will refuse;
But wanting you, my life is death;
   Nay, death Ild rather chuse!

"Content thy self, my dearest love;
   Thy rest at home shall bee
In Englandes sweet and pleasant isle;
   For travell fits not thee.

Faire ladies brooke not bloodye warres;
    Soft peace their sexe delights;
Not rugged campes, but courtlye bowers;
    Gay feastes, not cruell fights.'

My Rose shall safely here abide,
    With musicke passe the daye;
Whilst I, amonge the piercing pikes,
    My foes seeke far awaye.

My Rose shall shine in pearle, and golde,
    Whilst Ime in armour dighte;
Gay galliards here my love shall dance,
    Whilst I my foes goe fighte.

And you, Sir Thomas, whom I truste
    To bee my loves defence;
Be careful of my gallant Rose
    When I am parted hence."

And therewithall he fetcht a sigh,
    As though his heart would breake:
And Rosamonde, for very grief,
    Not one plaine word could speake.

And at their parting well they mighte
    In heart be grieved sore:
After that daye faire Rosamonde
    The king did see no more.

For when his grace had past the seas,
    And into France was gone;

With envious heart, Queene Ellinor,
    To Woodstocke came anone.

And forth she calls this trustye knighte,
    In an unhappy houre;
Who with his clue of twined thread,
    Came from this famous bower.

And when that they had wounded him,
    The queene this thread did gette,
And went where Ladye Rosamonde
    Was like an angell sette.

But when the queene with stedfast eye
    Beheld her beauteous face,
She was amazed in her minde
    At her exceeding grace.

Cast off from thee those robes, she said,
    That riche and costlye bee;
And drinke thou up this deadlye draught,
    Which I have brought to thee.

Then presentlye upon her knees
    Sweet Rosamonde did fall;
And pardon of the queene she crav'd
    For her offences all.

"Take pitty on my youthfull yeares,"
    Faire Rosamonde did crye;
"And lett mee not with poison stronge
    Enforced bee to dye.

I will renounce my sinfull life,
    And in some cloyster bide;
Or else be banisht, if you please,
    To range the world soe wide.

And for the fault which I have done,
    Though I was forc'd thereto,
Preserve my life, and punish mee
    As you thinke meet to doe."

And with these words, her lillie handes
    She wrunge full often there;
And downe along her lovely face
    Did trickle many a teare.

But nothing could this furious queene
    Therewith appeased bee;
The cup of deadlye poyson stronge,
    As she knelt on her knee,

Shee gave this comelye dame to drinke;
    Who tooke it in her hand,
And from her bended knee arose,
    And on her feet did stand:

And casting up her eyes to heaven,
    She did for mercye calle;
And drinking up the poison stronge,
    Her life she lost withalle.

And when that death through everye limbe
    Had showde its greatest spite,

Her chiefest foes did plaine confesse
    Shee was a glorious wight.

Her body then they did entomb,
    When life was fled away,
At Godstowe, neare to Oxford towne,
    As may be scene this day.

ROBIN HOOD AND GUY OF GISBORNE

When shaws beene sheene, and shradds full fayre,
    And leaves both large and longe,
Itt is merrye walking in the fayre forrest
    To heare the small birdes songe.

The woodweele sang, and wold not cease,
    Sitting upon the spraye,
Soe lowde, he wakened Robin Hood,
    In the greenwood where he lay.

Now by my faye, sayd jollye Robin,
    A sweaven I had this night;
I dreamt me of tow wighty yemen,
    That fast with me can fight.

Methought they did mee beate and binde,
    And tooke my bow mee froe;

If I be Robin alive in this lande,
    He be wroken on them towe.

Sweavens are swift, Master, quoth John,
    As the wind that blowes ore a hill;
For if itt be never so loude this night,
    To-morrow itt may be still.

Buske yee, bowne yee, my merry men all,
    And John shall goe with mee,
For Ile goe seeke yond wight yeomen,
    In greenwood where the bee.

Then the cast on their gownes of grene,
    And tooke theyr bowes each one;
And they away to the greene forrest
    A shooting forth are gone;

Until they came to the merry greenwood,
    Where they had gladdest bee,
There were the ware of a wight yeoman,
    His body leaned to a tree.

A sword and a dagger he wore by his side,
    Of manye a man the bane;
And he was clad in his capull hyde
    Topp and tayll and mayne.

Stand you still, master, quoth Litle John,
    Under this tree so grene,
And I will go to yond wight yeoman
    To know what he doth meane.

Ah! John, by me thou settest noe store,
    And that I farley finde:
How offt send I my men beffore
    And tarry my selfe behinde?

It is no cunning a knave to ken,
    And a man but heare him speake;
And itt were not for bursting of my bowe.
    John, I thy head wold breake.

As often wordes they breeden bale,
    So they parted Robin and John;
And John is gone to Barnesdale;
    The gates he knoweth eche one.

But when he came to Barnesdale,
    Great heavinesse there hee hadd,
For he found tow of his owne fellowes
    Were slaine both in a slade.

And Scarlette he was flyinge a-foote
    Fast over stocke and stone,
For the sheriffe with seven score men
    Fast after him is gone.

One shoote now I will shoote, quoth John,
    With Christ his might and mayne:
Ile make yond fellow that flyes soe fast,
    To stopp he shall be fayne.

Then John bent up his long bende-bowe,
    And fetteled him to shoote:

The bow was made of a tender boughe,
    And fell down to his foote.

Woe worth, woe worth thee, wicked wood,
    That ere thou grew on a tree;
For now this day thou art my bale,
    My boote when thou shold bee.

His shoote it was but loosely shott,
    Yet flewe not the arrowe in vaine,
For itt mett one of the sheriffes men,
    Good William a Trent was slaine.

It had bene better of William a Trent
    To have bene abed with sorrowe,
Than to be that day in the green wood slade
    To meet with Little Johns arrowe.

But as it is said, when men be mett
    Fyve can doe more than three,
The sheriffe hath taken little John,
    And bound him fast to a tree.

Thou shalt be drawen by dale and downe,
    And hanged hye on a hill.
But thou mayst fayle of thy purpose, quoth John,
    If itt be Christ his will.

Let us leave talking of Little John,
    And thinke of Robin Hood,
How he is gone to the wight yeoman,
    Where under the leaves he stood.

Good morrowe, good fellowe, sayd Robin so fayre,
    Good morrowe, good fellow, quoth he:
Methinkes by this bowe thou beares in thy hande
    A good archere thou sholdst bee.

I am wilfull of my waye, quo' the yeman,
    And of my morning tyde.
He lead thee through the wood, sayd Robin;
    Good fellow, He be thy guide.

I seeke an outlawe, the straunger sayd,
    Men call him Robin Hood;
Rather Ild meet with that proud outlawe,
    Than fortye pound so good.

Now come with me, thou wighty yeman,
    And Robin thou soone shalt see:
But first let us some pastime find
    Under the greenwood tree.

First let us some masterye make
    Among the woods so even,
Wee may chance to meet with Robin Hood
    Here att some unsett steven.

They cut them downe two summer shroggs,
    That grew both under a breere,
And sett them threescore rood in twaine
    To shoot the prickes y-fere:

Lead on, good fellowe, quoth Robin Hood,
    Lead on, I doe bidd thee.

Nay by my faith, good fellowe, hee sayd,
  My leader thou shalt bee.

The first time Robin shot at the pricke,
  He mist but an inch it froe:
The yeoman he was an archer good,
  But he cold never shoote soe.

The second shoote had the wightye yeman,
  He shote within the garlande:
But Robin he shott far better than hee,
  For he clave the good pricke wande.

A blessing upon thy heart, he sayd;
  Good fellowe, thy shooting is goode;
For an thy hart be as good as thy hand,
  Thou wert better then Robin Hoode.

Now tell me thy name, good fellowe, sayd he,
  Under the leaves of lyne.
Nay by my faith, quoth bolde Robin,
  Till thou have told me thine.

I dwell by dale and downe, quoth hee,
  And Robin to take Ime sworne;
And when I am called by my right name
  I am Guye of good Gisborne.

My dwelling is in this wood, sayes Robin,
  By thee I set right nought:
I am Robin Hood of Barnesdale,
  Whom thou so long hast sought.

He that hath neither beene kithe nor kin,
   Might have scene a full fayre sight,
To see how together these yeomen went
   With blades both browne and bright.

To see how these yeomen together they fought
   Two howres of a summers day:
Yet neither Robin Hood nor Sir Guy
   Them fettled to flye away.

Robin was reachles on a roote,
   And stumbled at that tyde;
And Guy was quick and nimble with-all,
   And hitt him ore the left side.

Ah deere Lady, sayd Robin Hood, 'thou
   That art both mother and may,'
I think it was never mans destinye
   To dye before his day.

Robin thought on our ladye deere,
   And soone leapt up againe,
And strait he came with a 'backward' stroke,
   And he Sir Guy hath slayne.

He took Sir Guys head by the hayre,
   And sticked itt on his bowes end:
Thou hast beene a traytor all thy liffe,
   Which thing must have an ende.

Robin pulled forth an Irish kniffe,
   And nicked Sir Guy in the face,

That he was never on woman born,
  Cold tell whose head it was.

Saies, Lye there, lye there, now Sir Guye,
  And with me be not wrothe,
If thou have had the worst stroked at my hand,
  Thou shalt have the better clothe.

Robin did off his gowne of greene,
  And on Sir Guy did it throwe,
And hee put on that capull hyde,
  That cladd him topp to toe.

The bowe, the arrowes, and litle home,
  Now with me I will beare;
For I will away to Barnesdale,
  To see how my men doe fare.

Robin Hood sett Guyes horne to his mouth.
  And a loud blast in it did blow.
That beheard the sheriffe of Nottingham,
  As he leaned under a lowe.

Hearken, hearken, sayd the sheriffe,
  I heare now tydings good,
For yonder I heare Sir Guyes horne blowe,
  And he hath slaine Robin Hoode.

Yonder I heare Sir Guyes home blowe,
  Itt blowes soe well in tyde,
And yonder comes that wightye yeoman,
  Cladd in his capull hyde.

Come hyther, come hyther, thou good Sir Guy,
　　Aske what thou wilt of mee.
O I will none of thy gold, sayd Robin,
　　Nor I will none of thy fee:

But now I have slaine the master, he sayes,
　　Let me go strike the knave;
This is all the rewarde I aske;
　　Nor noe other will I have.

Thou art a madman, said the sheriffe,
　　Thou sholdest have had a knights fee:
But seeing thy asking hath beene soe bad,
　　Well granted it shale be.

When Litle John heard his master speake,
　　Well knewe he it was his steven:
Now shall I be looset, quoth Litle John,
　　With Christ his might in heaven.

Fast Robin hee hyed him to Litle John,
　　He thought to loose him belive;
The sheriffe and all his companye
　　Fast after him did drive.
Stand abacke, stand abacke, sayd Robin;
　　Why draw you mee soe neere?
Itt was never the use in our countrye,
　　Ones shrift another shold heere.

But Robin pulled forth an Irysh kniffe,
　　And losed John hand and foote,

And gave him Sir Guyes bow into his hand,
    And bade it be his boote.

Then John he took Guyes bow in his hand,
    His boltes and arrowes eche one:
When the sheriffe saw Little John bend his bow,
    He fettled him to be gone.

Towards his house in Nottingham towne
    He fled full fast away;
And soe did all his companye:
    Not one behind wold stay.

But he cold neither runne soe fast,
    Nor away soe fast cold ryde,
But Litle John with an arrowe soe broad
    He shott him into the 'back'-syde.

THE BOY & THE MANTLE

The Boy and the Mantle

In Carleile dwelt King Arthur,
　A prince of passing might;

And there maintain'd his table round,
   Beset with many a knight.

And there he kept his Christmas
   With mirth and princely cheare,
When, lo! a straunge and cunning boy
   Before him did appeare.

A kirtle and a mantle
   This boy had him upon,
With brooches, rings, and owches,
   Full daintily bedone.

He had a sarke of silk
   About his middle meet;
And thus, with seemely curtesy,
   He did King Arthur greet.

"God speed thee, brave King Arthur,
   Thus feasting in thy bowre;
And Guenever thy goodly queen,
   That fair and peerlesse flowre.

"Ye gallant lords, and lordings,
   I wish you all take heed,
Lest, what ye deem a blooming rose,
   Should prove a cankred weed."

Then straitway from his bosome
   A little wand he drew;
And with it eke a mantle
   Of wondrous shape and hew.

"Now have you here, King Arthur,
Have this here of mee,
And give unto thy comely queen,
All-shapen as you see.

"No wife it shall become,
    That once hath been to blame."
Then every knight in Arthur's court
    Slye glaunced at his dame.

And first came Lady Guenever,
    The mantle she must trye.
This dame, she was new-fangled,
    And of a roving eye.

When she had tane the mantle,
    And all was with it cladde,
From top to toe it shiver'd down,
    As tho' with sheers beshradde.

One while it was too long,
    Another while too short,
And wrinkled on her shoulders
    In most unseemly sort.

Now green, now red it seemed,
    Then all of sable hue.
"Beshrew me," quoth King Arthur,
    "I think thou beest not true."

Down she threw the mantle,
    Ne longer would not stay;

But, storming like a fury,
　　To her chamber flung away.

She curst the whoreson weaver,
　　That had the mantle wrought:
And doubly curst the froward impe,
　　Who thither had it brought.

"I had rather live in desarts
　　Beneath the green-wood tree;
Than here, base king, among thy groomes,
　　The sport of them and thee."

Sir Kay call'd forth his lady,
　　And bade her to come near:
"Yet, dame, if thou be guilty,
　　I pray thee now forbear."

This lady, pertly gigling,
　　With forward step came on,
And boldly to the little boy
　　With fearless face is gone.

When she had tane the mantle,
　　With purpose for to wear;
It shrunk up to her shoulder,
　　And left her b——side bare.

Then every merry knight,
　　That was in Arthur's court,
Gib'd, and laught, and flouted,
　　To see that pleasant sport.

Downe she threw the mantle,
  No longer bold or gay,
But with a face all pale and wan,
  To her chamber slunk away.

Then forth came an old knight,
  A pattering o'er his creed;
And proffer'd to the little boy
  Five nobles to his meed;

"And all the time of Christmass
  Plumb-porridge shall be thine,
If thou wilt let my lady fair
  Within the mantle shine."

A saint his lady seemed,
  With step demure and slow,
And gravely to the mantle
  With mincing pace doth goe.

When she the same had taken,
  That was so fine and thin,
It shrivell'd all about her,
  And show'd her dainty skin.

Ah! little did HER mincing,
  Or HIS long prayers bestead;
She had no more hung on her,
  Than a tassel and a thread.

Down she threwe the mantle,
  With terror and dismay,

And, with a face of scarlet,
   To her chamber hyed away.

Sir Cradock call'd his lady,
   And bade her to come neare:
"Come, win this mantle, lady,
   And do me credit here.

"Come, win this mantle, lady,
   For now it shall be thine,
If thou hast never done amiss,
   Sith first I made thee mine."

The lady, gently blushing,
   With modest grace came on,
And now to trye the wondrous charm
   Courageously is gone.

When she had tane the mantle,
   And put it on her backe,
About the hem it seemed
   To wrinkle and to cracke.

"Lye still," shee cryed, "O mantle!
   And shame me not for nought,
I'll freely own whate'er amiss,
   Or blameful I have wrought.

"Once I kist Sir Cradocke
   Beneathe the green-wood tree:
Once I kist Sir Cradocke's mouth
   Before he married mee."

When thus she had her shriven,
   And her worst fault had told,
The mantle soon became her
   Right comely as it shold.

Most rich and fair of colour,
   Like gold it glittering shone:
And much the knights in Arthur's court
   Admir'd her every one.

Then towards King Arthur's table
   The boy he turn'd his eye:
Where stood a boar's head garnished
   With bayes and rosemarye.

When thrice he o'er the boar's head
   His little wand had drawne,
Quoth he, "There's never a cuckold's knife
   Can carve this head of brawne."

Then some their whittles rubbed
   On whetstone, and on hone:
Some threwe them under the table,
   And swore that they had none.

Sir Cradock had a little knife,
   Of steel and iron made;
And in an instant thro' the skull
   He thrust the shining blade.

He thrust the shining blade
   Full easily and fast;

And every knight in Arthur's court
    A morsel had to taste.

The boy brought forth a horne,
    All golden was the rim:
Saith he, "No cuckolde ever can
    Set mouth unto the brim.

"No cuckold can this little horne
    Lift fairly to his head;
But or on this, or that side,
    He shall the liquor shed."

Some shed it on their shoulder,
    Some shed it on their thigh;
And hee that could not hit his mouth,
    Was sure to hit his eye.

Thus he, that was a cuckold,
    Was known of every man:
But Cradock lifted easily,
    And wan the golden can.

Thus boar's head, horn and mantle,
    Were this fair couple's meed:
And all such constant lovers,
    God send them well to speed.

Then down in rage came Guenever,
    And thus could spightful say,
"Sir Cradock's wife most wrongfully
    Hath borne the prize away.

"See yonder shameless woman,
    That makes herselfe so clean:
Yet from her pillow taken
    Thrice five gallants have been.

"Priests, clarkes, and wedded men,
    Have her lewd pillow prest:
Yet she the wonderous prize forsooth
    Must beare from all the rest."

Then bespake the little boy,
    Who had the same in hold:
"Chastize thy wife, King Arthur,
    Of speech she is too bold:

"Of speech she is too bold,
    Of carriage all too free;
Sir King, she hath within thy hall
    A cuckold made of thee.

"All frolick light and wanton
    She hath her carriage borne:
And given thee for a kingly crown
    To wear a cuckold's horne."

THE HEIR OF LINNE

PART THE FIRST

Lithe and listen, gentlemen,
   To sing a song I will beginne:
It is of a lord of faire Scotland,
   Which was the unthrifty heire of Linne.

His father was a right good lord,
   His mother a lady of high degree;
But they, alas! were dead, him froe,
   And he lov'd keeping companie.

To spend the daye with merry cheare,
   To drinke and revell every night,
To card and dice from eve to morne,
   It was, I ween, his hearts delighte.

To ride, to runne, to rant, to roare,
    To alwaye spend and never spare,
I wott, an' it were the king himselfe,
    Of gold and fee he mote be bare.

Soe fares the unthrifty lord of Linne
    Till all his gold is gone and spent;
And he maun sell his landes so broad,
    His house, and landes, and all his rent.

His father had a keen stewarde,
    And John o' the Scales was called hee:
But John is become a gentel-man,
    And John has gott both gold and fee.

Sayes, Welcome, welcome, lord of Linne,
    Let nought disturb thy merry cheere;
Iff thou wilt sell thy landes soe broad,
    Good store of gold Ile give thee heere,

My gold is gone, my money is spent;
    My lande nowe take it unto thee:
Give me the golde, good John o' the Scales,
    And thine for aye my lande shall bee.

Then John he did him to record draw,
    And John he cast him a gods-pennie;
But for every pounde that John agreed,
    The lande, I wis, was well worth three.

He told him the gold upon the borde,
    He was right glad his land to winne;

The gold is thine, the land is mine,
  And now Ile be the lord of Linne.

Thus he hath sold his land soe broad,
  Both hill and holt, and moore and fenne,
All but a poore and lonesome lodge,
  That stood far off in a lonely glenne.

For soe he to his father hight.
  My sonne, when I am gonne, sayd hee,
Then thou wilt spend thy land so broad,
  And thou wilt spend thy gold so free:

But sweare me nowe upon the roode,
  That lonesome lodge thou'lt never spend;
For when all the world doth frown on thee,
  Thou there shalt find a faithful friend.

The heire of Linne is full of golde:
  And come with me, my friends, sayd hee,
Let's drinke, and rant, and merry make,
  And he that spares, ne'er mote he thee.

They ranted, drank, and merry made,
  Till all his gold it waxed thinne;
And then his friendes they slunk away;
  They left the unthrifty heire of Linne.

He had never a penny in his purse,
  Never a penny left but three,
And one was brass, another was lead,
  And another it was white money.

Nowe well-aday, sayd the heire of Linne,
　　Nowe well-aday, and woe is mee,
For when I was the lord of Linne,
　　I never wanted gold nor fee.

But many a trustye friend have I,
　　And why shold I feel dole or care?
Ile borrow of them all by turnes,
　　Soe need I not be never bare.

But one, I wis, was not at home;
　　Another had payd his gold away;
Another call'd him thriftless loone,
　　And bade him sharpely wend his way.

Now well-aday, sayd the heire of Linne,
　　Now well-aday, and woe is me;
For when I had my landes so broad,
　　On me they liv'd right merrilee.

To beg my bread from door to door
　　I wis, it were a brenning shame:
To rob and steale it were a sinne:
　　To worke my limbs I cannot frame.

Now Ile away to lonesome lodge,
　　For there my father bade me wend;
When all the world should frown on mee
　　I there shold find a trusty friend.

PART THE SECOND

Away then hyed the heire of Linne
   Oer hill and holt, and moor and fenne,
Untill he came to lonesome lodge,
   That stood so lowe in a lonely glenne.

He looked up, he looked downe,
   In hope some comfort for to winne:
But bare and lothly were the walles.
   Here's sorry cheare, quo' the heire of Linne.

The little windowe dim and darke
   Was hung with ivy, brere, and yewe;
No shimmering sunn here ever shone;
   No halesome breeze here ever blew.

No chair, ne table he mote spye,
   No cheerful hearth, ne welcome bed,
Nought save a rope with renning noose,
   That dangling hung up o'er his head.

And over it in broad letters,
   These words were written so plain to see:
"Ah! gracelesse wretch, hast spent thine all,
   And brought thyselfe to penurie?

"All this my boding mind misgave,
   I therefore left this trusty friend:
Let it now sheeld thy foule disgrace,
   And all thy shame and sorrows end."

Sorely shent wi' this rebuke,
    Sorely shent was the heire of Linne,
His heart, I wis, was near to brast
    With guilt and sorrowe, shame and sinne.

Never a word spake the heire of Linne,
    Never a word he spake but three:
"This is a trusty friend indeed,
    And is right welcome unto mee."

Then round his necke the corde he drewe,
    And sprung aloft with his bodie:
When lo! the ceiling burst in twaine,
    And to the ground came tumbling hee.

Astonyed lay the heire of Linne,
    Ne knewe if he were live or dead:
At length he looked, and saw a bille,
    And in it a key of gold so redd.

He took the bill, and lookt it on,
    Strait good comfort found he there:
It told him of a hole in the wall,
    In which there stood three chests in-fere.

Two were full of the beaten golde,
    The third was full of white money;
And over them in broad letters
    These words were written so plaine to see:

"Once more, my sonne, I sette thee clere;
    Amend thy life and follies past;

For but thou amend thee of thy life,
    That rope must be thy end at last."

And let it bee, sayd the heire of Linne;
    And let it bee, but if I amend:
For here I will make mine avow,
    This reade shall guide me to the end.

Away then went with a merry cheare,
    Away then went the heire of Linne;
I wis, he neither ceas'd ne blanne,
    Till John o' the Scales house he did winne.

And when he came to John o' the Scales,
    Upp at the speere then looked hee;
There sate three lords upon a rowe,
    Were drinking of the wine so free.

And John himself sate at the bord-head,
    Because now lord of Linne was hee.
I pray thee, he said, good John o' the Scales,
    One forty pence for to lend mee.

Away, away, thou thriftless loone;
    Away, away, this may not bee:
For Christs curse on my head, he sayd,
    If ever I trust thee one pennie.

Then bespake the heire of Linne,
    To John o' the Scales wife then spake he:
Madame, some almes on me bestowe,
    I pray for sweet Saint Charitie.

Away, away, thou thriftless loone,
    I swear thou gettest no almes of mee;
For if we shold hang any losel heere,
    The first we wold begin with thee.

Then bespake a good fellowe,
    Which sat at John o' the Scales his bord
Sayd, Turn againe, thou heire of Linne;
    Some time thou wast a well good lord;

Some time a good fellow thou hast been,
    And sparedst not thy gold nor fee;
Therefore He lend thee forty pence,
    And other forty if need bee.

And ever, I pray thee, John o' the Scales,
    To let him sit in thy companie:
For well I wot thou hadst his land,
    And a good bargain it was to thee.

Up then spake him John o' the Scales,
    All wood he answer'd him againe:
Now Christs curse on my head, he sayd,
    But I did lose by that bargaine.

And here I proffer thee, heire of Linne,
    Before these lords so faire and free,
Thou shalt have it backe again better cheape,
    By a hundred markes, than I had it of thee.

I draw you to record, lords, he said.
    With that he cast him a gods pennie:

Now by my fay, sayd the heire of Linne,
   And here, good John, is thy money.

And he pull'd forth three bagges of gold,
   And layd them down upon the bord:
All woe begone was John o' the Scales,
   Soe shent he cold say never a word.

He told him forth the good red gold,
   He told it forth with mickle dinne.
The gold is thine, the land is mine,
   And now Ime againe the lord of Linne.

Sayes, Have thou here, thou good fellowe,
   Forty pence thou didst lend me:
Now I am againe the lord of Linne,
   And forty pounds I will give thee.

He make the keeper of my forrest,
   Both of the wild deere and the tame;
For but I reward thy bounteous heart,
   I wis, good fellowe, I were to blame.

Now welladay! sayth Joan o' the Scales:
   Now welladay! and woe is my life!
Yesterday I was lady of Linne,
   Now Ime but John o' the Scales his wife.

Now fare thee well, sayd the heire of Linne;
    Farewell now, John o' the Scales, said hee:
Christs curse light on me, if ever again
    I bring my lands in jeopardy.

KING COPHETUA AND THE
BEGGAR MAID

I Read that once in Affrica
  A princely wight did raine,
Who had to name Cophetua,

As poets they did faine:
From natures lawes he did decline,
For sure he was not of my mind.
He cared not for women-kinde,
    But did them all disdaine.
But, marke, what hapened on a day,
As he out of his window lay,
He saw a beggar all in gray,
    The which did cause his paine.

The blinded boy, that shootes so trim,
    From heaven downe did hie;
He drew a dart and shot at him,
    In place where he did lye:
Which soone did pierse him to the quicke.
And when he felt the arrow pricke,
Which in his tender heart did sticke,
    He looketh as he would dye.
What sudden chance is this, quoth he,
That I to love must subject be,
Which never thereto would agree,
    But still did it defie?

Then from the window he did come,
    And laid him on his bed,
A thousand heapes of care did runne
    Within his troubled head:
For now he meanes to crave her love,
And now he seekes which way to proove
How he his fancie might remoove,
    And not this beggar wed.
But Cupid had him so in snare,

That this poor begger must prepare
A salve to cure him of his care,
    Or els he would be dead.

And, as he musing thus did lye,
    He thought for to devise
How he might have her companye,
    That so did 'maze his eyes.
In thee, quoth he, doth rest my life;
For surely thou shalt be my wife,
Or else this hand with bloody knife
    The Gods shall sure suffice.
Then from his bed he soon arose,
And to his pallace gate he goes;
Full little then this begger knowes
    When she the king espies.

The Gods preserve your majesty,
    The beggers all gan cry:
Vouchsafe to give your charity
    Our childrens food to buy.
The king to them his pursse did cast,
    And they to part it made great haste;
This silly woman was the last
    That after them did hye.
The king he cal'd her back againe,
And unto her he gave his chaine;
And said, With us you shal remaine
    Till such time as we dye:

For thou, quoth he, shalt be my wife,
    And honoured for my queene;

With thee I meane to lead my life,
    As shortly shall be seene:
Our wedding shall appointed be,
And every thing in its degree:
Come on, quoth he, and follow me,
    Thou shalt go shift thee cleane.
What is thy name, faire maid? quoth he.
Penelophon, O king, quoth she;
With that she made a lowe courtsey;
    A trim one as I weene.

Thus hand in hand along they walke
    Unto the king's pallace:
The king with curteous comly talke
    This beggar doth imbrace:
The begger blusheth scarlet red,
And straight againe as pale as lead,
But not a word at all she said,
    She was in such amaze.
At last she spake with trembling voyce,
And said, O king, I doe rejoyce
That you wil take me from your choyce,
    And my degree's so base.

And when the wedding day was come,
    The king commanded strait
The noblemen both all and some
    Upon the queene to wait.
And she behaved herself that day,
As if she had never walkt the way;
She had forgot her gown of gray,
    Which she did weare of late.

The proverbe old is come to passe,
The priest, when he begins his masse,
Forgets that ever clerke he was;
   He knowth not his estate.

Here you may read, Cophetua,
   Though long time fancie-fed,
Compelled by the blinded boy
   The begger for to wed:
He that did lovers lookes disdaine,
To do the same was glad and faine,
Or else he would himselfe have slaine,
In storie, as we read.
   Disdaine no whit, O lady deere,
   But pitty now thy servant heere,
   Least that it hap to thee this yeare,
      As to that king it did.

And thus they led a quiet life
   Duringe their princely raigne;
And in a tombe were buried both,
   As writers sheweth plaine.
The lords they tooke it grievously,
The ladies tooke it heavily,
The commons cryed pitiously,
   Their death to them was paine,
   Their fame did sound so passingly,

That it did pierce the starry sky,
And throughout all the world did flye
    To every princes realme.

SIR ANDREW BARTON

'When Flora with her fragrant flowers
  Bedeckt the earth so trim and gaye,
And Neptune with his daintye showers
  Came to present the monthe of Maye;'
King Henrye rode to take the ayre,
  Over the river of Thames past hee;
When eighty merchants of London came,
  And downe they knelt upon their knee.

"O yee are welcome, rich merchants;
  Good saylors, welcome unto mee."
They swore by the rood, they were saylors good,
  But rich merchants they cold not bee:
"To France nor Flanders dare we pass:
  Nor Bourdeaux voyage dare we fare;
And all for a rover that lyes on the seas,
  Who robbs us of our merchant ware."

King Henrye frowned, and turned him rounde,
  And swore by the Lord, that was mickle of might,
"I thought he had not beene in the world,
  Durst have wrought England such unright."
The merchants sighed, and said, alas!
  And thus they did their answer frame,
He is a proud Scott, that robbs on the seas,
  And Sir Andrewe Barton is his name.

The king lookt over his left shoulder,
  And an angrye look then looked hee:
"Have I never a lorde in all my realme,
  Will feitch yond tray tor unto me?"
Yea, that dare I; Lord Howard sayes;
  Yea, that dare I with heart and hand;
If it please your grace to give me leave,
  Myselfe wil be the only man.

Thou art but yong; the kyng replyed:
  Yond Scott hath numbered manye a yeare.
"Trust me, my liege, lie make him quail,
  Or before my prince I will never appeare."
Then bowemen and gunners thou shalt have,
  And chuse them over my realme so free;
Besides good mariners, and shipp-boyes,
  To guide the great shipp on the sea.

The first man, that Lord Howard chose,
  Was the ablest gunner in all the realm,
Thoughe he was three score yeeres and ten;
  Good Peter Simon was his name.
Peter, sais hee, I must to the sea,

To bring home a traytor live or dead:
Before all others I have chosen thee;
    Of a hundred gunners to be the head.

If you, my lord, have chosen mee
    Of a hundred gunners to be the head,
Then hang me up on your maine-mast tree,
    If I misse my marke one shilling bread.
My lord then chose a boweman rare,
    "Whose active hands had gained fame."
In Yorkshire was this gentleman borne,
    And William Horseley was his name.

Horseley, said he, I must with speede
    Go seeke a traytor on the sea,
And now of a hundred bowemen brave
    To be the head I have chosen thee.
If you, quoth hee, have chosen mee
    Of a hundred bowemen to be the head
On your main-mast He hanged bee,
    If I miss twelvescore one penny bread.

With pikes and gunnes, and bowemen bold,
    This noble Howard is gone to the sea;
With a valyant heart and a pleasant cheare,
    Out at Thames mouth sayled he.
And days he scant had sayled three,
    Upon the 'voyage,' he tooke in hand,
But there he mett with a noble shipp,
    And stoutely made itt stay and stand.

Thou must tell me, Lord Howard said,
　　Now who thou art, and what's thy name;
And shewe me where they dwelling is:
　　And whither bound, and whence thou came.
My name is Henry Hunt, quoth hee
　　With a heavye heart, and a carefull mind;
I and my shipp doe both belong
　　To the Newcastle, that stands upon Tyne.

Hast thou not heard, nowe, Henrye Hunt,
　　As thou hast sayled by daye and by night,
Of a Scottish rover on the seas;
　　Men call him Sir Andrew Barton, knight!
Then ever he sighed, and said alas!
　　With a grieved mind, and well away!
But over-well I knowe that wight,
　　I was his prisoner yesterday.

As I was sayling uppon the sea,
　　A Burdeaux voyage for to fare;
To his hach-borde he clasped me,
　　And robd me of all my merchant ware:
And mickle debts, God wot, I owe,
　　And every man will have his owne;
And I am nowe to London bounde,
　　Of our gracious king to beg a boone.

That shall not need, Lord Howard sais;
　　Lett me but once that robber see,
For every penny tane thee froe
　　It shall be doubled shillings three.
Nowe God forefend, the merchant said,

That you should seek soe far amisse!
God keepe you out of that traitors hands!
   Full litle ye wott what a man hee is.

Hee is brasse within, and steele without,
   With beames on his topcastle stronge;
And eighteen pieces of ordinance
   He carries on each side along:
And he hath a pinnace deerlye dight,
   St. Andrewes crosse that is his guide;
His pinnace beareth ninescore men,
   And fifteen canons on each side.

Were ye twentye shippes, and he but one;
   I sweare by kirke, and bower, and hall;
He wold overcome them everye one,
   If once his beames they doe downe fall.
This is cold comfort, sais my lord,
   To wellcome a stranger thus to the sea:
Yet He bring him and his ship to shore,
   Or to Scottland hee shall carrye mee.

Then a noble gunner you must have,
   And he must aim well with his ee,
And sinke his pinnace into the sea,
   Or else hee never orecome will bee:
And if you chance his shipp to borde,
   This counsel I must give withall,
Let no man to his topcastle goe
   To strive to let his beams downe fall.

And seven pieces of ordinance,
 I pray your honour lend to mee,
On each side of my shipp along,
 And I will lead you on the sea.
A glasse He sett, that may be seene
 Whether you sail by day or night;
And to-morrowe, I sweare, by nine of the clocke
 You shall meet with Sir Andrewe Barton knight.

THE SECOND PART

The merchant sett my lorde a glasse
 Soe well apparent in his sight,
And on the morrowe, by nine of the clocke,
 He shewed him Sir Andrewe Barton knight.
His hachebord it was 'gilt' with gold,
 Soe deerlye dight it dazzled the ee:
Nowe by my faith, Lord Howarde sais,
 This is a gallant sight to see.

Take in your ancyents, standards eke,
 So close that no man may them see;
And put me forth a white willowe wand,
 As merchants use to sayle the sea.
But they stirred neither top, nor mast;
 Stoutly they past Sir Andrew by.
What English churles are yonder, he sayd,
 That can soe little curtesye?

Now by the roode, three yeares and more
 I have beene admirall over the sea;

And never an English nor Portingall
　　Without my leave can passe this way.
Then called he forth his stout pinnace;
　　"Fetch backe yond pedlars nowe to mee:
I sweare by the masse, yon English churles
　　Shall all hang att my maine-mast tree."

With that the pinnace itt shot off,
　　Full well Lord Howard might it ken;
For itt stroke down my lord's fore mast,
　　And killed fourteen of his men.
Come hither, Simon, sayes my lord,
　　Looke that thy word be true, thou said;
For at my maine-mast thou shalt hang,
　　If thou misse thy marke one shilling bread.

Simon was old, but his heart itt was bold;
　　His ordinance he laid right lowe;
He put in chaine full nine yardes long,
　　With other great shott lesse, and moe;
And he lette goe his great gunnes shott:
　　Soe well he settled itt with his ee,
The first sight that Sir Andrew sawe,
　　He see his pinnace sunke in the sea.

And when he saw his pinnace sunke,
　　Lord, how his heart with rage did swell!
"Nowe cutt my ropes, itt is time to be gon;
　　Ile fetch yond pedlars backe mysell."
When my lord sawe Sir Andrewe loose,
　　Within his heart he was full faine:

"Now spread your ancyents, strike up your drummes,
    Sound all your trumpetts out amaine."

Fight on, my men, Sir Andrewe sais,
    Weale howsoever this geere will sway;
Itt is my Lord Admirall of England,
    Is come to seeke mee on the sea.
Simon had a sonne, who shott right well,
    That did Sir Andrewe mickle scare;
In att his decke he gave a shott,
    Killed threescore of his men of warre.

Then Henrye Hunt with rigour hott
    Came bravely on the other side,
Soone he drove downe his fore-mast tree,
    And killed fourscore men beside.
Nowe, out alas! Sir Andrewe cryed,
    What may a man now thinke, or say?
Yonder merchant theefe, that pierceth mee,
    He was my prisoner yesterday.

Come hither to me, thou Gordon good,
    That aye wast readye att my call:
I will give thee three hundred markes,
    If thou wilt let my beames downe fall.
Lord Howard hee then calld in haste,
    "Horseley see thou be true in stead;
For thou shalt at the maine-mast hang,
    If thou misse twelvescore one penny bread."

Then Gordon swarved the maine-mast tree,
    He swarved it with might and maine;

But Horseley with a bearing arrowe,
   Stroke the Gordon through the braine;
And he fell unto the haches again,
   And sore his deadlye wounde did bleed:
Then word went through Sir Andrews men,
   How that the Gordon hee was dead.

Come hither to mee, James Hambilton,
   Thou art my only sisters sonne,
If thou wilt let my beames downe fall
   Six hundred nobles thou hast wonne.
With that he swarved the maine-mast tree,
   He swarved it with nimble art;
But Horseley with a broad arrowe
   Pierced the Hambilton thorough the heart:

And downe he fell upon the deck,
   That with his blood did streame amaine:
Then every Scott cryed, Well-away!
   Alas! a comelye youth is slaine.
All woe begone was Sir Andrew then,
   With griefe and rage his heart did swell:
"Go fetch me forth my armour of proofe,
   For I will to the topcastle mysell."

"Goe fetch me forth my armour of proofe;
   That gilded is with gold soe cleare:
God be with my brother John of Barton!
   Against the Portingalls hee it ware;
And when he had on this armour of proofe,
   He was a gallant sight to see:

Ah! nere didst thou meet with living wight,
   My deere brother, could cope with thee."

Come hither Horseley, says my lord,
   And looke your shaft that itt goe right,
Shoot a good shoote in time of need,
   And for it thou shalt be made a knight.
Ile shoot my best, quoth Horseley then,
   Your honour shall see, with might and maine;
But if I were hanged at your maine-mast,
   I have now left but arrowes twaine.

Sir Andrew he did swarve the tree,
With right good will he swarved then:
Upon his breast did Horseley hitt,
   But the arrow bounded back agen.
Then Horseley spyed a privye place
   With a perfect eye in a secrette part;
Under the spole of his right arme
   He smote Sir Andrew to the heart.

"Fight on, my men," Sir Andrew sayes,
   "A little Ime hurt, but yett not slaine;
He but lye downe and bleede a while,
   And then He rise and fight againe.
Fight on, my men," Sir Andrew sayes,
   "And never flinch before the foe;
And stand fast by St. Andrewes crosse
   Until you heare my whistle blowe."

They never heard his whistle blow—
   Which made their hearts waxe sore adread:

Then Horseley sayd, Aboard, my lord,
    For well I wott Sir Andrew's dead.
They boarded then his noble shipp,
    They boarded it with might and maine;
Eighteen score Scots alive they found,
    The rest were either maimed or slaine.

Lord Howard tooke a sword in hand,
    And off he smote Sir Andrewes head,
"I must have left England many a daye,
    If thou wert alive as thou art dead."
He caused his body to be cast
    Over the hatchboard into the sea,
And about his middle three hundred crownes:
    "Wherever thou land this will bury thee."

Thus from the warres Lord Howard came,
    And backe he sayled ore the maine,
With mickle joy and triumphing
    Into Thames mouth he came againe.
Lord Howard then a letter wrote,
    And sealed it with scale and ring;
"Such a noble prize have I brought to your grace,
    As never did subject to a king:

"Sir Andrewes shipp I bring with mee;
    A braver shipp was never none:
Nowe hath your grace two shipps of warr,
    Before in England was but one."
King Henryes grace with royall cheere
    Welcomed the noble Howard home,

And where, said he, is this rover stout,
That I myselfe may give the doome?

"The rover, he is safe, my liege,
    Full many a fadom in the sea;
If he were alive as he is dead,
    I must have left England many a day:
And your grace may thank four men i' the ship
    For the victory wee have wonne,
These are William Horseley, Henry Hunt,
    And Peter Simon, and his sonne."

To Henry Hunt, the king then sayd,
    In lieu of what was from thee tane,
A noble a day now thou shalt have,
    Sir Andrewes jewels and his chayne.
And Horseley thou shalt be a knight,
    And lands and livings shalt have store;
Howard shall be erle Surrye hight,
    As Howards erst have beene before.

Nowe, Peter Simon, thou art old,
    I will maintaine thee and thy sonne:
And the men shall have five hundred markes
    For the good service they have done.
Then in came the queene with ladyes fair
    To see Sir Andrewe Barton knight:
They weend that hee were brought on shore,
    And thought to have seen a gallant sight.

But when they see his deadlye face,
    And eyes soe hollow in his head,

I wold give, quoth the king, a thousand markes,
   This man were alive as hee is dead:
Yett for the manfull part hee playd,
   Which fought soe well with heart and hand,
His men shall have twelvepence a day,
   Till they come to my brother kings high land.

MAY COLLIN

May Collin

May Collin . . .

   . . . was her father's heir,

And she fell in love with a false priest,

   And she rued it ever mair.

He followd her butt, he followd her benn,
  He followd her through the hall,
Till she had neither tongue nor teeth
  Nor lips to say him naw.

"We'll take the steed out where he is,
  The gold where eer it be,
And we'll away to some unco land,
  And married we shall be."

They had not riden a mile, a mile,
  A mile but barely three,
Till they came to a rank river,
  Was raging like the sea.

"Light off, light off now, May Collin,
  It's here that you must die;
Here I have drownd seven king's daughters,
  The eight now you must be.

"Cast off, cast off now, May Collin,
  Your gown that's of the green;
For it's oer good and oer costly
  To rot in the sea-stream.

"Cast off, cast off now, May Collin,
  Your coat that's of the black;
For it's oer good and oer costly
  To rot in the sea-wreck.

"Cast off, cast off now, May Collin,
  Your stays that are well laced;

For thei'r oer good and costly
   In the sea's ground to waste.

"Cast [off, cast off now, May Collin,]
   Your sark that's of the holland;
For [it's oer good and oer costly]
   To rot in the sea-bottom."

"Turn you about now, falsh Mess John,
   To the green leaf of the tree;
It does not fit a mansworn man
   A naked woman to see."

He turnd him quickly round about,
   To the green leaf of the tree;
She took him hastly in her arms
   And flung him in the sea.

"Now lye you there, you falsh Mess John,
   My mallasin go with thee!
You thought to drown me naked and bare,
   But take your cloaths with thee,
And if there be seven king's daughters there
   Bear you them company"

She lap on her milk steed
   And fast she bent the way,
And she was at her father's yate
   Three long hours or day.

Up and speaks the wylie parrot,
   So wylily and slee:

"Where is the man now, May Collin,
  That gaed away wie thee?"

"Hold your tongue, my wylie parrot,
  And tell no tales of me,
And where I gave a pickle befor
  It's now I'll give you three."

THE BLIND BEGGAR'S DAUGHTER
OF BEDNALL GREEN

PART THE FIRST

Itt was a blind beggar, had long lost his sight,
He had a faire daughter of bewty most bright;
And many a gallant brave suiter had shee,
For none was soe comelye as pretty Bessee.

And though shee was of favour most faire,
Yett seeing shee was but a poor beggars heyre,
Of ancyent housekeepers despised was shee,
Whose sonnes came as suitors to prettye Bessee.

Wherefore in great sorrow faire Bessy did say,
Good father, and mother, let me goe away

To seeke out my fortune, whatever itt bee.
This suite then they granted to prettye Bessee.

Then Bessy, that was of bewtye soe bright,
All cladd in gray russett, and late in the night
From father and mother alone parted shee;
Who sighed and sobbed for prettye Bessee.

Shee went till shee came to Stratford-le-Bow;
Then knew shee not whither, nor which way to goe:
With teares shee lamented her hard destinie,
So sadd and soe heavy was pretty Bessee.

Shee kept on her journey untill it was day,
And went unto Rumford along the hye way;
Where at the Queenes armes entertained was shee;
Soe faire and wel favoured was pretty Bessee.

Shee had not beene there a month to an end,
But master and mistress and all was her friend:
And every brave gallant, that once did her see,
Was straight-way enamoured of pretty Bessee.

Great gifts they did send her of silver and gold,
And in their songs daylye her love was extold;
Her beawtye was blazed in every degree;
Soe faire and soe comelye was pretty Bessee.

The young men of Rumford in her had their joy;
Shee shewed herself curteous, and modestlye coye;
And at her commandment still wold they bee;
Soe fayre and soe comlye was pretty Bessee.

Foure suitors att once unto her did goe;
They craved her favor, but still she sayd noe;
I wold not wish gentles to marry with mee.
Yett ever they honored prettye Bessee.

The first of them was a gallant young knight,
And he came unto her disguisde in the night;
The second a gentleman of good degree,
Who wooed and sued for prettye Bessee.

A merchant of London, whose wealth was not small,
He was the third suiter, and proper withall:
Her masters own sonne the fourth man must bee,
Who swore he would dye for pretty Bessee.

And, if thou wilt marry with mee, quoth the knight,
Ile make thee a ladye with joy and delight;
My hart's so inthralled by thy bewtle,
That soone I shall dye for prettye Bessee.

The gentleman sayd, Come, marry with mee,
As fine as a ladye my Bessy shal bee:
My life is distressed: O heare me, quoth hee;
And grant me thy love, my prettye Bessee.

Let me bee thy husband, the merchant cold say,
Thou shalt live in London both gallant and gay;
My shippes shall bring home rych jewells for thee,
And I will for ever love pretty Bessee.

Then Bessy shee sighed, and thus she did say,
My father and mother I meane to obey;

First gett their good will, and be faithfull to mee,
And you shall enjoye your prettye Bessee.

To every one this answer shee made,
Wherfore unto her they joyfullye sayd,
This thing to fulfill wee all doe agree;
But where dwells thy father, my prettye Besse?

My father, shee said, is soone to be seene:
The seely blind beggar of Bednall-greene,
That daylye sits begging for charitie,
He is the good father of pretty Bessee.

His markes and his tokens are knowen very well;
He always is led with a dogg and a bell:
A seely olde man, God knoweth, is hee,
Yett hee is the father of pretty Bessee.

Nay then, quoth the merchant, thou art not for mee:
Nor, quoth the innholder, my wiffe thou shalt bee:
I lothe, sayd the gentle, a beggars degree,
And therefore, adewe, my pretty Bessee!

Why then, quoth the knight, hap better or worse,
I waighe not true love by the waight of my pursse,
And bewtye is bewtye in every degree;
Then welcome unto me, my prettye Bessee.

With thee to thy father forthwith I will goe.
Nay soft, quoth his kinsmen, it must not be soe;
A poor beggars daughter noe ladye shal bee,
Then take thy adew of pretty Bessee.

But soone after this, by breake of the day,
The knight had from Rumford stole Bessy away.
The younge men of Rumford, as thicke might bee,
Rode after to feitch againe pretty Bessee.

As swifte as the winde to ryde they were scene,
Untill they came neare unto Bednall-greene;
And as the knight lighted most courteouslie,
They all fought against him for pretty Bessee.

But rescew came speedilye over the plaine,
Or else the young knight for his love had been slaine.
This fray being ended, then straitway he see
His kinsmen come rayling at pretty Bessee.

Then spake the blind beggar, Although I bee poore,
Yett rayle not against my child at my own doore:
Though shee be not decked in velvett and pearle,
Yett will I dropp angells with you for my girle.

And then, if my gold may better her birthe,
And equall the gold that you lay on the earth,
Then neyther rayle nor grudge you to see
The blind beggars daughter a lady to bee.

But first you shall promise, and have it well knowne,
The gold that you drop shall all be your owne.
With that they replyed, Contented bee wee.
Then here's, quoth the beggar, for pretty Bessee.

With that an angell he cast on the ground,
And dropped in angels full three thousand pound;

And oftentime itt was proved most plaine,
For the gentlemens one the beggar droppt twayne:

Soe that the place, wherin they did sitt,
With gold it was covered every whitt.
The gentlemen then having dropt all their store,
Sayd, Now, beggar, hold, for wee have noe more.

Thou hast fulfilled thy promise arright.
Then marry, quoth he, my girle to this knight;
And heere, added hee, I will now throwe you downe
A hundred pounds more to buy her a gowne.

The gentlemen all, that this treasure had seene,
Admired the beggar of Bednall-greene:
And all those, that were her suitors before,
Their fleshe for very anger they tore.

Thus was faire Besse matched to the knight,
And then made a ladye in others despite:
A fairer ladye there never was seene,
Than the blind beggars daughter of Bednall-greene.

But of their sumptuous marriage and feast,
What brave lords and knights thither were prest,
The SECOND FITT shall set forth to your sight
With marveilous pleasure, and wished delight.

PART THE SECOND

Off a blind beggars daughter most bright,
That late was betrothed unto a younge knight;
All the discourse therof you did see;
But now comes the wedding of pretty Bessee.

Within a gorgeous palace most brave,
Adorned with all the cost they cold have,
This wedding was kept most sumptuouslie,
And all for the credit of pretty Bessee.

All kind of dainties, and delicates sweete
Were bought for the banquet, as it was most meete;
Partridge, and plover, and venison most free,
Against the brave wedding of pretty Bessee.

This marriage through England was spread by report,
Soe that a great number therto did resort
Of nobles and gentles in every degree;
And all for the fame of prettye Bessee.

To church then went this gallant younge knight;
His bride followed after, an angell most bright,
With troopes of ladyes, the like nere was scene
As went with sweete Bessy of Bednall-greene.

This marryage being solempnized then,
With musicke performed by the skilfullest men,
The nobles and gentles sate downe at that tyde,
Each one admiring the beautiful bryde.

Now, after the sumptuous dinner was done,
To talke, and to reason a number begunn:
They talkt of the blind beggars daughter most bright,
And what with his daughter he gave to the knight.

Then spake the nobles, "Much marveil have wee,
This jolly blind beggar wee cannot here see."
My lords, quoth the bride, my father's so base,
He is loth with his presence these states to disgrace.

"The prayse of a woman in question to bringe
Before her own face, were a flattering thinge;
But wee thinke thy father's baseness," quoth they,
"Might by thy bewtye be cleane put awaye."

They had noe sooner these pleasant words spoke,
But in comes the beggar cladd in a silke cloke;
A faire velvet capp, and a fether had hee,
And now a musicyan forsooth he wold bee.

He had a daintye lute under his arme,
He touched the strings, which made such a charme,
Saies, Please you to heare any musicke of mee,
Ile sing you a song of pretty Bessee.

With that his lute he twanged straightway,
And thereon begann most sweetlye to play;
And after that lessons were playd two or three,
He strayn'd out this song most delicatelie.

"A poore beggars daughter did dwell on a greene,
Who for her fairenesse might well be a queene:

A blithe bonny lasse, and a daintye was shee,
And many one called her pretty Bessee.

"Her father hee had noe goods, nor noe land,
But begged for a penny all day with his hand;
And yett to her marriage he gave thousands three,
And still he hath somewhat for pretty Bessee.

"And if any one here her birth doe disdaine,
Her father is ready, with might and with maine,
To proove shee is come of noble degree:
Therfore never flout att prettye Bessee."

With that the lords and the companye round
With harty laughter were readye to swound;
Att last said the lords, Full well wee may see,
The bride and the beggar's behoulden to thee.

On this the bride all blushing did rise,
The pearlie dropps standing within her faire eyes,
O pardon my father, grave nobles, quoth shee,
That throughe blind affection thus doteth on mee.

If this be thy father, the nobles did say,
Well may he be proud of this happy day;
Yett by his countenance well may wee see,
His birth and his fortune did never agree:

And therefore, blind man, we pray thee bewray,
(and looke that the truth thou to us doe say)
Thy birth and thy parentage, whatt itt may bee;
For the love that thou bearest to pretty Bessee.

"Then give me leave, nobles and gentles, each one,
One song more to sing, and then I have done;
And if that itt may not winn good report,
Then doe not give me a GROAT for my sport.

"Sir Simon de Montfort my subject shal bee;
Once chiefe of all the great barons was hee,
Yet fortune so cruelle this lorde did abase,
Now loste and forgotten are hee and his race.

"When the barons in armes did King Henrye oppose,
Sir Simon de Montfort their leader they chose;
A leader of courage undaunted was hee,
And oft-times he made their enemyes flee.

"At length in the battle on Eveshame plaine
The barons were routed, and Montford was slaine;
Moste fatall that battel did prove unto thee,
Thoughe thou wast not borne then, my prettye Bessee!

"Along with the nobles, that fell at that tyde,
His eldest son Henrye, who fought by his side,
Was fellde by a blowe, he receivde in the fight!
A blowe that deprivde him for ever of sight.

"Among the dead bodyes all lifeless he laye,
Till evening drewe on of the following daye,
When by a yong ladye discovered was hee;
And this was thy mother, my prettye Bessee!

"A barons faire daughter stept forth in the nighte
To search for her father, who fell in the fight,

And seeing young Montfort, where gasping he laye,
Was moved with pitye, and brought him awaye.

"In secrette she nurst him, and swaged his paine,
While he throughe the realme was beleeved to be slaine
At lengthe his faire bride she consented to bee,
And made him glad father of prettye Bessee.

"And nowe lest oure foes our lives sholde betraye,
We clothed ourselves in beggars arraye;
Her jewelles shee solde, and hither came wee:
All our comfort and care was our prettye Bessee.

"And here have we lived in fortunes despite,
Thoughe poore, yet contented with humble delighte:
Full forty winters thus have I beene
A silly blind beggar of Bednall-greene.

"And here, noble lordes, is ended the song
Of one, that once to your own ranke did belong:
And thus have you learned a secrette from mee,
That ne'er had been knowne, but for prettye Bessee."

Now when the faire companye everye one,
Had heard the strange tale in the song he had showne,
They all were amazed, as well they might bee,
Both at the blinde beggar, and pretty Bessee.

With that the faire bride they all did embrace,
Saying, Sure thou art come of an honourable race,
Thy father likewise is of noble degree,
And thou art well worthy a lady to bee.

Thus was the feast ended with joye and delighte,
A bridegroome most happy then was the younge knighte,
In joy and felicitie long lived hee,
All with his faire ladye, the pretty Bessee.

THOMAS THE RHYMER

Thomas lay on the Huntlie bank,
  A spying ferlies wi his eee,

And he did spy a lady gay,
    Come riding down by the lang lee.

Her steed was o the dapple grey,
    And at its mane there hung bells nine;
He thought he heard that lady say,
    "They gowden bells sall a' be thine."

Her mantle was o velvet green,
    And a' set round wi jewels fine;
Her hawk and hounds were at her side,
    And her bugle-horn wi gowd did shine.

Thomas took aff baith cloak and cap,
    For to salute this gay lady:
"O save ye, save ye, fair Queen o Heavn,
    And ay weel met ye save and see!"

"I'm no the Queen o Heavn, Thomas;
    I never carried my head sae hee;
For I am but a lady gay,
    Come out to hunt in my follee.

"Now gin ye kiss my mouth, Thomas,
    Ye mauna miss my fair bodee;
Then ye may een gang hame and tell
    That ye've lain wi a gay ladee."

"O gin I loe a lady fair,
    Nae ill tales o her wad I tell,
And it's wi thee I fain wad gae,
    Tho it were een to heavn or hell."

"Then harp and carp, Thomas," she said,
  "Then harp and carp alang wi me;
But it will be seven years and a day
  Till ye win back to yere ain countrie."

The lady rade, True Thomas ran,
  Until they cam to a water wan;
O it was night, and nae delight,
  And Thomas wade aboon the knee.

It was dark night, and nae starn-light,
  And on they waded lang days three,
And they heard the roaring o a flood,
  And Thomas a waefou man was he.

Then they rade on, and farther on,
  Untill they came to a garden green;
To pu an apple he put up his hand,
  For the lack o food he was like to tyne.

"O haud yere hand, Thomas," she cried,
  "And let that green flourishing be;
For it's the very fruit o hell,
  Beguiles baith man and woman o yere countrie.

"But look afore ye, True Thomas,
  And I shall show ye ferlies three;
Yon is the gate leads to our land,
  Where thou and I sae soon shall be.

"And dinna ye see yon road, Thomas,
  That lies out-owr yon lilly lee?

Weel is the man yon gate may gang,
    For it leads him straight to the heavens hie.

"But do you see yon road, Thomas,
    That lies out-owr yon frosty fell?
Ill is the man yon gate may gang,
    For it leads him straight to the pit o hell.

"Now when ye come to our court, Thomas,
    See that a weel-learned man ye be;
For they will ask ye, one and all,
    But ye maun answer nane but me.

"And when nae answer they obtain,
    Then will they come and question me,
And I will answer them again
    That I gat yere aith at the Eildon tree.

*   *   *   *   *

"Ilka seven years, Thomas,
    We pay our teindings unto hell,
And ye're sae leesome and sae strang
    That I fear, Thomas, it will be yeresell."

YOUNG BEICHAN

In London city was Bicham born,
　He longd strange countries for to see,

But he was taen by a savage Moor,
  Who handld him right cruely.

For thro his shoulder he put a bore,
  An thro the bore has pitten a tree,
An he's gard him draw the carts o wine,
  Where horse and oxen had wont to be.

He's casten [him] in a dungeon deep,
  Where he coud neither hear nor see;
He's shut him up in a prison strong,
  An he's handld him right cruely.

O this Moor he had but ae daughter,
  I wot her name was Shusy Pye;
She's doen her to the prison-house,
  And she's calld Young Bicham one word

"O hae ye ony lands or rents,
  Or citys in your ain country,
Coud free you out of prison strong,
  An coud mantain a lady free?"

"O London city is my own,
  An other citys twa or three,
Coud loose me out o prison strong,
  An coud mantain a lady free."

O she has bribed her father's men
  Wi meikle goud and white money,
She's gotten the key o the prison doors,
  An she has set Young Bicham free.

She's g'in him a loaf o good white bread,
　　But an a flask o Spanish wine,
An she bad him mind on the ladie's love
　　That sae kindly freed him out o pine.

"Go set your foot on good ship-board,
　　An haste you back to your ain country,
An before that seven years has an end,
　　Come back again, love, and marry me."

It was long or seven years had an end
　　She longd fu sair her love to see;
She's set her foot on good ship-board,
　　And turnd her back on her ain country.

She's saild up, so has she doun,
　　Till she came to the other side;
She's landed at Young Bicham's gates,
　　An I hop this day she sal be his bride.

"Is this Young Bicham's gates?" says she,
　　"Or is that noble prince within?"
"He's up the stairs wi his bonny bride,
　　An monny a lord and lady wi him."

"O has he taen a bonny bride,
　　An has he clean forgotten me!"
An sighing said that gay lady,
　　I wish I were in my ain country!

But she's pitten her han in her pocket,
　　An gin the porter guineas three;

Says, Take ye that, ye proud porter,
   An bid the bridegroom speak to me.

O whan the porter came up the stair,
   He's fa'n low down upon his knee:
"Won up, won up, ye proud porter,
   An what makes a' this courtesy?"

"O I've been porter at your gates
   This mair nor seven years an three,
But there is a lady at them now
   The like of whom I never did see.

"For on every finger she has a ring,
   An on the mid-finger she has three,
An there's a meikle goud aboon her brow
   As woud buy an earldome o lan to me."

Then up it started Young Bicham,
   An sware so loud by Our Lady,
"It can be nane but Shusy Pye,
   That has come oer the sea to me."

O quickly ran he down the stair,
   O fifteen steps he has made but three;
He's tane his bonny love in his arms,
   An a wot he kissd her tenderly.

"O hae you tane a bonny bride?
   An hae you quite forsaken me?
An hae ye quite forgotten her
   That gae you life an liberty?"

142

She's lookit oer her left shoulder
   To hide the tears stood in her ee;
"Now fare thee well, Young Bicham," she says,
   "I'll strive to think nae mair on thee."

"Take back your daughter, madam," he says,
   "An a double dowry I'll gi her wi;
For I maun marry my first true love,
   That's done and suffered so much for me."

He's take his bonny love by the ban,
   And led her to yon fountain stane;
He's changd her name frae Shusy Pye,
   An he's cald her his bonny love, Lady Jane.

BRAVE LORD WILLOUGHBEY

The fifteenth day of July,
　　With glistering spear and shield,
A famous fight in Flanders
　　Was foughten in the field:
The most couragious officers
　　Were English captains three;
But the bravest man in battel
　　Was brave Lord Willoughbey.

The next was Captain Norris,
　　A valiant man was hee:
The other Captain Turner,
　　From field would never flee.
With fifteen hundred fighting men,
　　Alas! there were no more,

They fought with fourteen thousand then,
    Upon the bloody shore.

Stand to it, noble pikemen,
    And look you round about:
And shoot you right, you bow-men,
    And we will keep them out:
You musquet and calliver men,
    Do you prove true to me,
I'le be the formost man in fight,
    Says brave Lord Willoughbey.

And then the bloody enemy
    They fiercely did assail,
And fought it out most furiously,
    Not doubting to prevail:
The wounded men on both sides fell
    Most pitious for to see,
Yet nothing could the courage quell
    Of brave Lord Willoughbey.

For seven hours to all mens view
    This fight endured sore,
Until our men so feeble grew
    That they could fight no more;
And then upon dead horses
    Full savourly they eat,
And drank the puddle water,
    They could no better get.

When they had fed so freely,
    They kneeled on the ground,

And praised God devoutly
   For the favour they had found;
And beating up their colours,
   The fight they did renew,
And turning tow'rds the Spaniard,
   A thousand more they slew.

The sharp steel-pointed arrows,
   And bullets thick did fly,
Then did our valiant soldiers
   Charge on most furiously;
Which made the Spaniards waver,
   They thought it best to flee,
They fear'd the stout behaviour
   Of brave Lord Willoughbey.

Then quoth the Spanish general,
   Come let us march away,
I fear we shall be spoiled all
   If here we longer stay;
For yonder comes Lord Willoughbey
   With courage fierce and fell,
He will not give one inch of way
   For all the devils in hell.

And then the fearful enemy
   Was quickly put to flight,
Our men persued couragiously,
   And caught their forces quite;
But at last they gave a shout,
   Which ecchoed through the sky,

God, and St. George for England!
  The conquerors did cry.

This news was brought to England
  With all the speed might be,
And soon our gracious queen was told
  Of this same victory.
O this is brave Lord Willoughbey,
  My love that ever won,
Of all the lords of honour
  'Tis he great deeds hath done.

To the souldiers that were maimed,
  And wounded in the fray,
The queen allowed a pension
  Of fifteen pence a day;
And from all costs and charges
  She quit and set them free:
And this she did all for the sake
  Of brave Lord Willoughbey.

Then courage, noble Englishmen,
  And never be dismaid;
If that we be but one to ten,
  We will not be afraid
To fight with foraign enemies,
  And set our nation free.
And thus I end the bloody bout
  Of brave Lord Willoughbey.

THE SPANISH LADY'S LOVE

Will you hear a Spanish lady,
    How shed wooed an English man?
Garments gay and rich as may be
    Decked with jewels she had on.
Of a comely countenance and grace was she,
And by birth and parentage of high degree.

As his prisoner there he kept her,
    In his hands her life did lye!
Cupid's bands did tye them faster
    By the liking of an eye.
In his courteous company was all her joy,
To favour him in any thing she was not coy.

But at last there came commandment
    For to set the ladies free,

With their jewels still adorned,
    None to do them injury.
Then said this lady mild, Full woe is me;
O let me still sustain this kind captivity!

Gallant captain, shew some pity
    To a ladye in distresse;
Leave me not within this city,
    For to dye in heavinesse:
Thou hast this present day my body free,
But my heart in prison still remains with thee.

"How should'st thou, fair lady, love me,
    Whom thou knowest thy country's foe?
Thy fair wordes make me suspect thee:
    Serpents lie where flowers grow."
All the harme I wishe to thee, most courteous knight,
God grant the same upon my head may fully light.
Blessed be the time and season,
    That you came on Spanish ground;
If our foes you may be termed,
    Gentle foes we have you found:
With our city, you have won our hearts eche one,
Then to your country bear away, that is your owne.

"Rest you still, most gallant lady;
    Rest you still, and weep no more;
Of fair lovers there is plenty,
    Spain doth yield a wonderous store."
Spaniards fraught with jealousy we often find,
But Englishmen through all the world are counted kind.

Leave me not unto a Spaniard,
    You alone enjoy my heart:
I am lovely, young, and tender,
    Love is likewise my desert:
Still to serve thee day and night my mind is prest;
The wife of every Englishman is counted blest.
"It wold be a shame, fair lady,
    For to bear a woman hence;
English soldiers never carry
    Any such without offence."
I'll quickly change myself, if it be so,
And like a page He follow thee, where'er thou go.

"I have neither gold nor silver
    To maintain thee in this case,
And to travel is great charges,
    As you know in every place."
My chains and jewels every one shal be thy own,
And eke five hundred pounds in gold that lies unknown.

"On the seas are many dangers,
    Many storms do there arise,
Which wil be to ladies dreadful,
    And force tears from watery eyes."
Well in troth I shall endure extremity,
For I could find in heart to lose my life for thee.

"Courteous ladye, leave this fancy,
    Here comes all that breeds the strife;
I in England have already
    A sweet woman to my wife:

I will not falsify my vow for gold nor gain,
Nor yet for all the fairest dames that live in Spain."

O how happy is that woman
    That enjoys so true a friend!
Many happy days God send her;
    Of my suit I make an end:
On my knees I pardon crave for my offence,
Which did from love and true affection first commence.

Commend me to thy lovely lady,
    Bear to her this chain of gold;
And these bracelets for a token;
    Grieving that I was so bold:
All my jewels in like sort take thou with thee,
For they are fitting for thy wife, but not for me.

I will spend my days in prayer,
    Love and all her laws defye;
In a nunnery will I shroud mee
    Far from any companye:
But ere my prayers have an end, be sure of this,
To pray for thee and for thy love I will not miss.

Thus farewell, most gallant captain!
    Farewell too my heart's content!
Count not Spanish ladies wanton,
    Though to thee my love was bent:
Joy and true prosperity goe still with thee!
"The like fall ever to thy share, most fair ladie."

THE FRIAR OF ORDERS GRAY

It was a friar of orders gray
    Walkt forth to tell his beades;
And he met with a lady faire,
    Clad in a pilgrime's weedes.

Now Christ thee save, thou reverend friar,
    I pray thee tell to me,
If ever at yon holy shrine
    My true love thou didst see.

And how should I know your true love
    From many another one?
O by his cockle hat, and staff,
    And by his sandal shoone.

But chiefly by his face and mien,
    That were so fair to view;
His flaxen locks that sweetly curl'd,
    And eyne of lovely blue.

O lady, he is dead and gone!
　　Lady, he's dead and gone!
And at his head a green grass turfe,
　　And at his heels a stone.

Within these holy cloysters long
　　He languisht, and he dyed,
Lamenting of a ladyes love,
　　And 'playning of her pride.

Here bore him barefac'd on his bier
　　Six proper youths and tall,
And many a tear bedew'd his grave
　　Within yon kirk-yard wall.

And art thou dead, thou gentle youth!
　　And art thou dead and gone!
And didst thou die for love of me!
　　Break, cruel heart of stone!

O weep not, lady, weep not soe;
　　Some ghostly comfort seek:
Let not vain sorrow rive thy heart,
　　Ne teares bedew thy cheek.

O do not, do not, holy friar,
　　My sorrow now reprove;
For I have lost the sweetest youth,
　　That e'er wan ladyes love.

And nowe, alas! for thy sad losse,
　　I'll evermore weep and sigh;

For thee I only wisht to live,
    For thee I wish to dye.

Weep no more, lady, weep no more,
    Thy sorrowe is in vaine:
For violets pluckt the sweetest showers
    Will ne'er make grow againe.

Our joys as winged dreams doe flye,
    Why then should sorrow last?
Since grief but aggravates thy losse,
    Grieve not for what is past.

O say not soe, thou holy friar;
    I pray thee, say not soe:
For since my true-love dyed for mee,
    'Tis meet my tears should flow.

And will he ne'er come again?
    Will he ne'er come again?
Ah! no, he is dead and laid in his grave,
    For ever to remain.

His cheek was redder than the rose;
    The comliest youth was he!
But he is dead and laid in his grave:
    Alas, and woe is me!

Sigh no more, lady, sigh no more,
    Men were deceivers ever:
One foot on sea and one on land,
    To one thing constant never.

Hadst thou been fond, he had been false,
   And left thee sad and heavy;
For young men ever were fickle found,
   Since summer trees were leafy.

Now say not so, thou holy friar,
   I pray thee say not soe;
My love he had the truest heart:
   O he was ever true!

And art thou dead, thou much-lov'd youth,
   And didst thou dye for mee?
Then farewell home; for ever-more
   A pilgrim I will bee.

But first upon my true-loves grave
   My weary limbs I'll lay,
And thrice I'll kiss the green-grass turf,
   That wraps his breathless clay.

Yet stay, fair lady; rest awhile
   Beneath this cloyster wall:
See through the hawthorn blows the cold wind,
   And drizzly rain doth fall.

O stay me not, thou holy friar;
   O stay me not, I pray;
No drizzly rain that falls on me,
   Can wash my fault away.

Yet stay, fair lady, turn again,
   And dry those pearly tears;

For see beneath this gown of gray
  Thy own true-love appears.

Here forc'd by grief, and hopeless love,
  These holy weeds I sought;
And here amid these lonely walls
  To end my days I thought.

But haply for my year of grace
  Is not yet past away,
Might I still hope to win thy love,
  No longer would I stay.

Now farewell grief, and welcome joy
  Once more unto my heart;
For since I have found thee, lovely youth,
  We never more will part.

CLERK COLVILL

Clerk Colvill and his lusty dame
   Were walking in the garden green;

The belt around her stately waist
   Cost Clerk Colvill of pounds fifteen.

"O promise me now, Clerk Colvill,
   Or it will cost ye muckle strife,
Ride never by the wells of Slane,
   If ye wad live and brook your life."

"Now speak nae mair, my lusty dame,
   Now speak nae mair of that to me;
Did I neer see a fair woman,
   But I wad sin with her body?"

He's taen leave o his gay lady,
   Nought minding what his lady said,
And he's rode by the wells of Slane,
   Where washing was a bonny maid.

"Wash on, wash on, my bonny maid,
   That wash sae clean your sark of silk;"
"And weel fa you, fair gentleman,
   Your body whiter than the milk."

* * * *

Then loud, loud cry'd the Clerk Colvill,
   "O my head it pains me sair;"
"Then take, then take," the maiden said,
   "And frae my sark you'll cut a gare."

Then she's gied him a little bane-knife,
　　And frae her sark he cut a share;
She's ty'd it round his whey-white face,
　　But ay his head it aked mair.

Then louder cry'd the Clerk Colville,
　　"O sairer, sairer akes my head;"
"And sairer, sairer ever will,"
　　The maiden crys, "till you be dead."

Out then he drew his shining blade,
　　Thinking to stick her where she stood,
But she was vanished to a fish,
　　And swam far off, a fair mermaid.

"O mother, mother, braid my hair;
　　My lusty lady, make my bed;
O brother, take my sword and spear,
　　For I have seen the false mermaid."

SIR ALDINGAR

SIR ALDINGAR

Our king he kept a false stewarde,
   Sir Aldingar they him call;
A falser steward than he was one,
   Servde not in bower nor hall.

He wolde have layne by our comelye queene,
   Her deere worshippe to betraye:
Our queene she was a good woman,
   And evermore said him naye.

Sir Aldingar was wrothe in his mind,
   With her hee was never content,
Till traiterous meanes he colde devyse,
   In a fyer to have her brent.

There came a lazar to the kings gate,
   A lazar both blinde and lame:

He tooke the lazar upon his backe,
    Him on the queenes bed has layne.

"Lye still, lazar, whereas thou lyest,
    Looke thou goe not hence away;
He make thee a whole man and a sound
    In two howers of the day."

Then went him forth Sir Aldingar,
    And hyed him to our king:
"If I might have grace, as I have space,
    Sad tydings I could bring."

Say on, say on, Sir Aldingar,
    Saye on the soothe to mee.
"Our queene hath chosen a new new love,
    And shee will have none of thee.

"If shee had chosen a right good knight,
    The lesse had beene her shame;
But she hath chose her a lazar man,
    A lazar both blinde and lame."

If this be true, thou Aldingar,
    The tyding thou tellest to me,
Then will I make thee a rich rich knight,
    Rich both of golde and fee.

But if it be false, Sir Aldingar,
    As God nowe grant it bee!
Thy body, I sweare by the holye rood,
    Shall hang on the gallows tree.

He brought our king to the queenes chamber,
    And opend to him the dore.
A lodlye love, King Harry says,
    For our queene dame Elinore!

If thou were a man, as thou art none,
    Here on my sword thoust dye;
But a payre of new gallowes shall be built,
    And there shalt thou hang on hye.

Forth then hyed our king, I wysse,
    And an angry man was hee;
And soone he found Queen Elinore,
    That bride so bright of blee.

Now God you save, our queene, madame,
    And Christ you save and see;
Heere you have chosen a newe newe love,
    And you will have none of mee.

If you had chosen a right good knight,
    The lesse had been your shame;
But you have chose you a lazar man,
    A lazar both blinde and lame.

Therfore a fyer there shalt be built,
    And brent all shalt thou bee.—
Now out alacke! said our comly queene,
    Sir Aldingar's false to mee.

Now out alacke! sayd our comlye queene,
    My heart with griefe will brast.

I had thought swevens had never been true;
    I have proved them true at last.

I dreamt in my sweven on Thursday eve,
    In my bed whereas I laye.
I dreamt a grype and a grimlie beast
    Had carryed my crowne awaye;

My gorgett and my kirtle of golde,
    And all my faire head-geere:
And he wold worrye me with his tush
    And to his nest y-beare:

Saving there came a little 'gray' hawke,
    A merlin him they call,
Which untill the grounde did strike the grype,
    That dead he downe did fall.

Giffe I were a man, as now I am none,
    A battell wold I prove,
To fight with that traitor Aldingar,
    Att him I cast my glove.

But seeing Ime able noe battell to make,
    My liege, grant me a knight
To fight with that traitor Sir Aldingar,
    To maintaine me in my right.

"Now forty dayes I will give thee
    To seeke thee a knight therein:
If thou find not a knight in forty dayes
    Thy bodye it must brenn."

Then shee sent east, and shee sent west,
    By north and south bedeene:
But never a champion colde she find,
    Wolde fight with that knight soe keene.

Now twenty dayes were spent and gone,
    Noe helpe there might be had;
Many a teare shed our comelye queene
    And aye her hart was sad.

Then came one of the queenes damselles,
    And knelt upon her knee,
"Cheare up, cheare up, my gracious dame,
    I trust yet helpe may be:

And here I will make mine avowe,
    And with the same me binde;
That never will I return to thee,
    Till I some helpe may finde."

Then forth she rode on a faire palfraye
    Oer hill and dale about:
But never a champion colde she finde,
    Wolde fighte with that knight so stout.

And nowe the daye drewe on a pace,
    When our good queene must dye;
All woe-begone was that faire damselle,
    When she found no helpe was nye.

All woe-begone was that faire damselle,
    And the salt teares fell from her eye:

When lo! as she rode by a rivers side,
    She met with a tinye boye.

A tinye boye she mette, God wot,
    All clad in mantle of golde;
He seemed noe more in mans likenesse,
    Then a childe of four yeere old.

Why grieve you, damselle faire, he sayd,
    And what doth cause you moane?
The damsell scant wolde deigne a looke,
    But fast she pricked on.

Yet turne againe, thou faire damselle
    And greete thy queene from mee:
When bale is att hyest, boote is nyest,
    Nowe helpe enoughe may bee.

Bid her remember what she dreamt
    In her bedd, wheras shee laye;
How when the grype and grimly beast
    Wolde have carried her crowne awaye,

Even then there came the little gray hawke,
    And saved her from his clawes:
Then bidd the queene be merry at hart,
    For heaven will fende her cause.

Back then rode that faire damselle,
    And her hart it lept for glee:
And when she told her gracious dame
    A gladd woman then was shee:

But when the appointed day was come,
    No helpe appeared nye:
Then woeful, woeful was her hart,
    And the teares stood in her eye.

And nowe a fyer was built of wood;
    And a stake was made of tree;
And now Queene Elinor forth was led,
    A sorrowful sight to see.

Three times the herault he waved his hand,
    And three times spake on hye:
Giff any good knight will fende this dame,
    Come forth, or shee must dye.

No knight stood forth, no knight there came,
    No helpe appeared nye:
And now the fyer was lighted up,
    Queen Elinor she must dye.

And now the fyer was lighted up,
    As hot as hot might bee;
When riding upon a little white steed,
    The tinye boy they see.

"Away with that stake, away with those brands,
    And loose our comelye queene:
I am come to fight with Sir Aldingar,
    And prove him a traitor keene."

Forthe then stood Sir Aldingar,
    But when he saw the chylde,

He laughed, and scoffed, and turned his backe,
    And weened he had been beguylde.

"Now turne, now turne thee, Aldingar,
    And eyther fighte or flee;
I trust that I shall avenge the wronge,
    Thoughe I am so small to see."

The boy pulld forth a well good sworde
    So gilt it dazzled the ee;
The first stroke stricken at Aldingar,
    Smote off his leggs by the knee.

"Stand up, stand up, thou false traitor,
    And fight upon thy feete,
For and thou thrive, as thou begin'st,
    Of height wee shall be meete."

A priest, a priest, sayes Aldingar,
    While I am a man alive.
A priest, a priest, sayes Aldingar,
    Me for to houzle and shrive.

I wolde have laine by our comlie queene,
    Bot shee wolde never consent;
Then I thought to betraye her unto our kinge
    In a fyer to have her brent.

There came a lazar to the kings gates,
    A lazar both blind and lame:
I tooke the lazar upon my backe,
    And on her bedd had him layne.

Then ranne I to our comlye king,
 These tidings sore to tell.
But ever alacke! sayes Aldingar,
 Falsing never doth well.

Forgive, forgive me, queene, madame,
 The short time I must live.
"Nowe Christ forgive thee, Aldingar,
 As freely I forgive."

Here take thy queene, our king Harrye,
 And love her as thy life,
For never had a king in Christentye.
 A truer and fairer wife.

King Henrye ran to claspe his queene,
 And loosed her full sone:
Then turned to look for the tinye boye;
 —The boye was vanisht and gone.

But first he had touched the lazar man,
 And stroakt him with his hand:
The lazar under the gallowes tree
 All whole and sounde did stand.

The lazar under the gallowes tree
 Was comelye, straight and tall;
King Henrye made him his head stewarde
 To wayte withinn his hall.

EDOM O' GORDON

It fell about the Martinmas,
    Quhen the wind blew shril and cauld,
Said Edom o' Gordon to his men,
    We maun draw till a hauld.

And quhat a hauld sall we draw till,
    My mirry men and me?
We wul gae to the house o' the Rodes,
    To see that fair ladie.

The lady stude on her castle wa',
    Beheld baith dale and down:
There she was ware of a host of men
    Cum ryding towards the toun.

O see ze nat, my mirry men a'?
　　O see za nat quhat I see?
Methinks I see a host of men:
　　I marveil quha they be.

She weend it had been hir luvely lord,
　　As he cam ryding hame;
It was the traitor Edom o' Gordon,
　　Quha reckt nae sin nor shame.

She had nae sooner buskit hirsel,
　　And putten on hir goun,
But Edom o' Gordon and his men
　　Were round about the toun.

They had nae sooner supper sett,
　　Nae sooner said the grace,
But Edom o' Gordon and his men
　　Were light about the place.

The lady ran up to hir towir head,
　　Sa fast as she could hie,
To see if by hir fair speeches
　　She could wi' him agree.

But quhan he see this lady saif,
　　And hir yates all locked fast,
He fell into a rage of wrath,
　　And his look was all aghast.

Cum doun to me, ze lady gay,
　　Cum doun, cum doun to me:

This night sall ye lig within mine armes,
    To-morrow my bride sall be.

I winnae cum doun ze fals Gordon,
    I winnae cum doun to thee;
I winna forsake my ain dear lord,
    That is sae far frae me.

Give owre zour house, ze lady fair,
    Give owre zour house to me,
Or I sall brenn yoursel therein,
    Bot and zour babies three.

I winnae give owre, ze false Gordon,
    To nae sik traitor as zee;
And if ze brenn my ain dear babes,
    My lord sall make ze drie.

But reach my pistoll, Glaud my man,
    And charge ze weil my gun:
For, but an I pierce that bluidy butcher,
    My babes we been undone.

She stude upon hir castle wa',
    And let twa bullets flee:
She mist that bluidy butchers hart,
    And only raz'd his knee.

Set fire to the house, quo' fals Gordon,
    All wood wi' dule and ire:
Fals lady, ze sall rue this deid,
    As ze bren in the fire.

Wae worth, wae worth ze, Jock my man,
  I paid ze weil zour fee;
Quhy pu' ze out the ground-wa' stane,
  Lets in the reek to me?

And ein wae worth ze, Jock my man,
  I paid ze weil zour hire;
Quhy pu' ze out the ground-wa' stane,
  To me lets in the fire?

Ze paid me weil my hire, lady;
  Ze paid me weil my fee:
But now I'm Edom o' Gordons man,
  Maun either doe or die.

O than bespaik hir little son,
  Sate on the nurses knee:
Sayes, Mither deare, gi' owre this house,
  For the reek it smithers me.

I wad gie a' my gowd, my childe,
  Say wald I a' my fee,
For ane blast o' the western wind,
  To blaw the reek frae thee.

O then bespaik hir dochter dear,
  She was baith jimp and sma;
O row me in a pair o' sheits,
  And tow me owre the wa.

They rowd hir in a pair o' sheits,
  And towd hir owre the wa:

172

But on the point of Gordons spear
   She gat a deadly fa.

O bonnie bonnie was hir mouth,
   And cherry were her cheiks,
And clear clear was hir zellow hair,
   Whereon the reid bluid dreips.

Then wi' his spear he turnd hir owre,
   O gin hir face was wan!
He sayd, Ze are the first that eir
   I wisht alive again.

He turnd hir owre and owre againe,
   O gin hir skin was whyte!
I might ha spared that bonnie face
   To hae been sum mans delyte.

Busk and boun, my merry men a',
   For ill dooms I doe guess;
I cannae luik in that bonnie face,
   As it lyes on the grass.

Thame, luiks to freits, my master deir,
   Then freits wil follow thame:
Let neir be said brave Edom o' Gordon
   Was daunted by a dame.

But quhen the ladye see the fire
   Cum flaming owre hir head,
She wept and kist her children twain,
   Sayd, Bairns, we been but dead.

The Gordon then his bougill blew,
   And said, Awa', awa';
This house o' the Rodes is a' in flame,
   I hauld it time to ga'.

O then bespyed hir ain dear lord,
   As hee cam owr the lee;
He sied his castle all in blaze Sa far as he could see.

Then sair, O sair his mind misgave,
   And all his hart was wae;
Put on, put on, my wighty men,
   So fast as ze can gae.

Put on, put on, my wighty men,
   Sa fast as ze can drie;
For he that is hindmost of the thrang
   Sall neir get guid o' me.

Than sum they rade, and sum they rin,
   Fou fast out-owr the bent;
But eir the foremost could get up,
   Baith lady and babes were brent.

He wrang his hands, he rent his hair,
   And wept in teenefu' muid:
O traitors, for this cruel deid
   Ze sall weep tiers o' bluid.

And after the Gordon he is gane,
   Sa fast as he might drie.
And soon i' the Gordon's foul hartis bluid
   He's wroken his dear ladie.

CHEVY CHASE

God prosper long our noble king,
  Our lives and safetyes all;
A woefull hunting once there did
  In Chevy-Chace befall;

To drive the deere with hound and horne,
  Erle Percy took his way,
The child may rue that is unborne,
  The hunting of that day.

The stout Erle of Northumberland
  A vow to God did make,
His pleasure in the Scottish woods
  Three summers days to take;

The cheefest harts in Chevy-chace
    To kill and beare away.
These tydings to Erle Douglas came,
    In Scotland where he lay:

Who sent Erle Percy present word,
    He wold prevent his sport.
The English erle, not fearing that,
    Did to the woods resort

With fifteen hundred bow-men bold;
    All chosen men of might,
Who knew full well in time of neede
    To ayme their shafts arright.

The galland greyhounds swiftly ran,
    To chase the fallow deere:
On munday they began to hunt,
    Ere day-light did appeare;

And long before high noone they had
    An hundred fat buckes slaine;
Then having dined, the drovyers went
    To rouze the deare againe.

The bow-men mustered on the hills,
    Well able to endure;
Theire backsides all, with speciall care,
    That day were guarded sure.

The hounds ran swiftly through the woods,
    The nimble deere to take,
That with their cryes the hills and dales
    An eccho shrill did make.

Lord Percy to the quarry went,
    To view the slaughter'd deere;
Quoth he, Erle Douglas promised
    This day to meet me heere:

But if I thought he wold not come,
    Noe longer wold I stay.
With that, a brave younge gentleman
    Thus to the Erle did say:

Loe, yonder doth Erle Douglas come,
    His men in armour bright;
Full twenty hundred Scottish speres
    All marching in our sight;

All men of pleasant Tivydale,
    Fast by the river Tweede:
O cease your sports, Erle Percy said,
    And take your bowes with speede:

And now with me, my countrymen,
    Your courage forth advance;
For there was never champion yett,
    In Scotland nor in France,

That ever did on horsebacke come,
    But if my hap it were,

I durst encounter man for man,
    With him to break a spere.

Erle Douglas on his milke-white steede,
    Most like a baron bolde,
Rode foremost of his company,
    Whose armour shone like gold.

Show me, sayd hee, whose men you bee,
    That hunt soe boldly heere,
That, without my consent, doe chase
    And kill my fallow-deere.

The first man that did answer make
    Was noble Percy hee;
Who sayd, Wee list not to declare,
    Nor shew whose men wee bee:
Yet wee will spend our deerest blood,
    Thy cheefest harts to slay.
Then Douglas swore a solempne oathe,
    And thus in rage did say,

Ere thus I will out-braved bee,
    One of us two shall dye:
I know thee well, an erle thou art;
    Lord Percy, soe am I.

But trust me, Percy, pittye it were,
    And great offence to kill
Any of these our guiltlesse men,
    For they have done no ill.

Let thou and I the battell trye,
    And set our men aside.
Accurst bee he, Erle Percy sayd,
    By whome this is denyed.

Then stept a gallant squier forth,
    Witherington was his name,
Who said, I wold not have it told
    To Henry our king for shame,

That ere my captaine fought on foote,
    And I stood looking on.
You be two erles, sayd Witherington,
    And I a squier alone:

He doe the best that doe I may,
    While I have power to stand:
While I have power to weeld my sword
    He fight with hart and hand.

Our English archers bent their bowes,
    Their harts were good and trew;
Att the first flight of arrowes sent,
    Full four-score Scots they slew.

Yet bides Earl Douglas on the bent,
    As Chieftain stout and good.
As valiant Captain, all unmov'd
    The shock he firmly stood.

His host he parted had in three,
    As Leader ware and try'd,

And soon his spearmen on their foes
   Bare down on every side.

To drive the deere with hound and horne,
   Douglas bade on the bent
Two captaines moved with mickle might
   Their speres to shivers went.

Throughout the English archery
   They dealt full many a wound:
But still our valiant Englishmen
   All firmly kept their ground:

And throwing strait their bows away,
   They grasp'd their swords so bright:
And now sharp blows, a heavy shower,
   On shields and helmets light.

They closed full fast on every side,
   Noe slackness there was found:
And many a gallant gentleman
   Lay gasping on the ground.

O Christ! it was a griefe to see;
   And likewise for to heare,
The cries of men lying in their gore,
   And scattered here and there.

At last these two stout erles did meet,
   Like captaines of great might:
Like lyons wood, they layd on lode,
   And made a cruell fight:

They fought untill they both did sweat,
  With swords of tempered steele;
Untill the blood, like drops of rain,
  They tricklin downe did feele.

Yeeld thee, Lord Percy, Douglas sayd
  In faith I will thee bringe,
Where thou shalt high advanced bee
  By James our Scottish king:

Thy ransome I will freely give,
  And this report of thee,
Thou art the most couragious knight,
  That ever I did see.

Noe, Douglas, quoth Erle Percy then,
  Thy proffer I doe scorne;
I will not yeelde to any Scott,
  That ever yett was borne.

With that, there came an arrow keene
  Out of an English bow,
Which struck Erle Douglas to the heart,
  A deepe and deadlye blow:

Who never spake more words than these,
  Fight on, my merry men all;
For why, my life is at an end;
  Lord Percy sees my fall.

Then leaving liffe, Erie Percy tooke
  The dead man by the hand;

And said, Erle Douglas, for thy life
   Wold I had lost my land.

O Christ! my verry hart doth bleed
   With sorrow for thy sake;
For sure, a more redoubted knight
   Mischance cold never take.

A knight amongst the Scotts there was
   Which saw Erle Douglas dye,
Who streight in wrath did vow revenge
   Upon the Lord Percye:

Sir Hugh Mountgomery was he call'd,
   Who, with a spere most bright,
Well-mounted on a gallant steed,
   Ran fiercely through the fight;

And past the English archers all,
   Without all dread or feare;
And through Earl Percyes body then
   He thrust his hatefull spere;

With such a vehement force and might
   He did his body gore,
The staff ran through the other side
   A large cloth-yard and more.

So thus did both these nobles dye,
   Whose courage none could staine:
An English archer then perceiv'd
   The noble erle was slaine;

He had a bow bent in his hand,
    Made of a trusty tree;
An arrow of a cloth-yard long
    Up to the head drew hee:

Against Sir Hugh Mountgomerye,
    So right the shaft he sett,
The grey goose-winge that was thereon,
    In his harts bloode was wette.

This fight did last from breake of day,
    Till setting of the sun;
For when they rang the evening-bell,
    The battel scarce was done.

With stout Erle Percy there was slaine
    Sir John of Egerton,
Sir Robert Ratcliff, and Sir John,
    Sir James that bold barron:

And with Sir George and stout Sir James,
    Both knights of good account,
Good Sir Ralph Raby there was slaine,
    Whose prowesse did surmount.

For Witherington needs must I wayle,
    As one in doleful dumpes;
For when his leggs were smitten off,
    He fought upon his stumpes.

And with Erle Douglas, there was slaine
    Sir Hugh Montgomerye,

Sir Charles Murray, that from the feeld
      One foote wold never flee.

Sir Charles Murray, of Ratcliff, too,
      His sisters sonne was hee;
Sir David Lamb, so well esteem'd,
      Yet saved cold not bee.

And the Lord Maxwell in like case
      Did with Erle Douglas dye:
Of twenty hundred Scottish speres,
      Scarce fifty-five did flye.

Of fifteen hundred Englishmen,
      Went home but fifty-three;
The rest were slaine in Chevy-Chace,
      Under the greene woode tree.

Next day did many widowes come,
      Their husbands to bewayle;
They washt their wounds in brinish teares,
      But all wold not prevayle.

Theyr bodyes, bathed in purple gore,
      They bare with them away:
They kist them dead a thousand times,
      Ere they were cladd in clay.

The news was brought to Eddenborrow,
      Where Scotlands king did raigne,
That brave Erle Douglas suddenlye
      Was with an arrow slaine:

O heavy newes, King James did say,
 Scotland may witnesse bee,
I have not any captaine more
 Of such account as hee.

Like tydings to King Henry came,
 Within as short a space,
That Percy of Northumberland
 Was slaine in Chevy-Chace:

Now God be with him, said our king,
 Sith it will noe better bee;
I trust I have, within my realme,
 Five hundred as good as hee:

Yett shall not Scotts nor Scotland say,
 But I will vengeance take:
I'll be revenged on them all,
 For brave Erle Percyes sake.

This vow full well the king perform'd
 After, at Humbledowne;
In one day, fifty knights were slayne,
 With lords of great renowne:

And of the rest, of small acount,
 Did many thousands dye:
Thus endeth the hunting of Chevy-Chase,
 Made by the Erle Percy.

God save our king, and bless this land
    With plenty, joy, and peace;
And grant henceforth, that foule debate
    'Twixt noblemen may cease.

SIR LANCELOT DU LAKE

When Arthur first in court began,
   And was approved king,
By force of armes great victorys wanne,
   And conquest home did bring,

Then into England straight he came
   With fifty good and able
Knights, that resorted unto him,
   And were of his round table:

And he had justs and turnaments,
   Whereto were many prest,
Wherein some knights did far excell
   And eke surmount the rest.

But one Sir Lancelot du Lake,
    Who was approved well,
He for his deeds and feats of armes
    All others did excell.

When he had rested him a while,
    In play, and game, and sportt,
He said he wold goe prove himselfe
    In some adventurous sort.

He armed rode in a forrest wide,
    And met a damsell faire,
Who told him of adventures great,
    Whereto he gave great eare.

Such wold I find, quoth Lancelott:
    For that cause came I hither.
Thou seemest, quoth shee, a knight full good,
    And I will bring thee thither.

Wheras a mighty knight doth dwell,
    That now is of great fame:
Therefore tell me what wight thou art,
    And what may be thy name.

"My name is Lancelot du Lake."
    Quoth she, it likes me than:
Here dwelles a knight who never was
    Yet matcht with any man:

Who has in prison threescore knights
    And four, that he did wound;

Knights of King Arthurs court they be,
    And of his table round.

She brought him to a river side,
    And also to a tree,
Whereon a copper bason hung,
    And many shields to see.

He struck soe hard, the bason broke;
    And Tarquin soon he spyed:
Who drove a horse before him fast,
    Whereon a knight lay tyed.

Sir knight, then sayd Sir Lancelett,
    Bring me that horse-load hither,
And lay him downe, and let him rest;
    Weel try our force together:

For, as I understand, thou hast,
    So far as thou art able,
Done great despite and shame unto
    The knights of the Round Table.

If thou be of the Table Round,
    Quoth Tarquin speedilye,
Both thee and all thy fellowship
    I utterly defye.

That's over much, quoth Lancelott tho,
    Defend thee by and by.
They sett their speares unto their steeds,
    And eache att other flie.

They coucht theire speares (their horses ran,
    As though there had beene thunder),
And strucke them each immidst their shields,
    Wherewith they broke in sunder.

Their horsses backes brake under them,
    The knights were both astound:
To avoyd their horsses they made haste
    And light upon the ground.

They tooke them to their shields full fast,
    Their swords they drewe out than,
With mighty strokes most eagerlye
    Each at the other ran.

They wounded were, and bled full sore,
    They both for breath did stand,
And leaning on their swords awhile,
    Quoth Tarquine, Hold thy hand,

And tell to me what I shall aske.
    Say on, quoth Lancelot tho.
Thou art, quoth Tarquine, the best knight
    That ever I did know:

And like a knight, that I did hate:
    Soe that thou be not hee,
I will deliver all the rest,
    And eke accord with thee.

That is well said, quoth Lancelott;
    But sith it must be soe,

What knight is that thou hatest thus
　　I pray thee to me show.

His name is Lancelot du Lake,
　　He slew my brother deere;
Him I suspect of all the rest:
　　I would I had him here.

Thy wish thou hast, but yet unknowne,
　　I am Lancelot du Lake,
Now knight of Arthurs Table Round;
　　King Hauds son of Schuwake;

And I desire thee to do thy worst.
　　Ho, ho, quoth Tarquin tho'
One of us two shall ende our lives
　　Before that we do go.

If thou be Lancelot du Lake,
　　Then welcome shalt thou bee:
Wherfore see thou thyself defend,
　　For now defye I thee.

They buckled them together so,
　　Like unto wild boares rashing;
And with their swords and shields they ran
　　At one another slashing:

The ground besprinkled was with blood:
　　Tarquin began to yield;
For he gave backe for wearinesse,
　　And lowe did beare his shield.

This soone Sir Lancelot espyde,
    He leapt upon him then,
He pull'd him downe upon his knee,
    And rushing off his helm,

Forthwith he strucke his necke in two,
    And, when he had soe done,
From prison threescore knights and four
    Delivered everye one.

GIL MORRICE

Gil Morrice was an erles son,
  His name it waxed wide;
  It was nae for his great riches,

Nor zet his mickle pride;
Bot it was for a lady gay,
   That livd on Carron side.

Quhair sail I get a bonny boy,
   That will win hose and shoen;
That will gae to Lord Barnards ha',
   And bid his lady cum?
And ze maun rin my errand, Willie;
   And ze may rin wi' pride;
Quhen other boys gae on their foot
   On horse-back ze sail ride.

O no! Oh no! my master dear!
   I dare nae for my life;
I'll no gae to the bauld barons,
   For to triest furth his wife.
My bird Willie, my boy Willie;
   My dear Willie, he sayd:
How can ze strive against the stream?
   For I sall be obeyd.

Bot, O my master dear! he cryd,
   In grene wod ze're zour lain;
Gi owre sic thochts, I walde ze rede,
   For fear ze should be tain.
Haste, haste, I say, gae to the ha',
   Bid hir cum here wi speid:
If ze refuse my heigh command,
   Ill gar zour body bleid.

Gae bid hir take this gay mantel,
  'Tis a' gowd hot the hem;
Bid hir cum to the gude grene wode,
  And bring nane bot hir lain:
And there it is a silken sarke,
  Hir ain hand sewd the sleive;
And bid hir cum to Gill Morice,
  Speir nae bauld barons leave.

Yes, I will gae zour black errand,
  Though it be to zour cost;
Sen ze by me will nae be warn'd,
  In it ze sail find frost.
The baron he is a man of might,
  He neir could bide to taunt,
As ze will see before its nicht,
  How sma' ze hae to vaunt.

And sen I maun zour errand rin
  Sae sair against my will,
I'se mak a vow and keip it trow,
  It sall be done for ill.
And quhen he came to broken brigue,
  He bent his bow and swam;
And quhen he came to grass growing,
  Set down his feet and ran.

And quhen he came to Barnards ha',
  Would neither chap nor ca':
Bot set his bent bow to his breist,
  And lichtly lap the wa'.
He wauld nae tell the man his errand,

Though he stude at the gait;
Bot straiht into the ha' he cam,
   Quhair they were set at meit.

Hail! hail! my gentle sire and dame!
   My message winna waite;
Dame, ze maun to the gude grene wod
   Before that it be late.
Ze're bidden tak this gay mantel,
   Tis a' gowd bot the hem:
Zou maun gae to the gude grene wode,
   Ev'n by your sel alane.

And there it is, a silken sarke,
   Your ain hand sewd the sleive;
Ze maun gae speik to Gill Morice:
   Speir nae bauld barons leave.
The lady stamped wi' hir foot,
   And winked wi' hir ee;
Bot a' that she coud say or do,
   Forbidden he wad nae bee.

Its surely to my bow'r-woman;
   It neir could be to me.
I brocht it to Lord Barnards lady;
   I trow that ze be she.
Then up and spack the wylie nurse,
   (The bairn upon hir knee)
If it be cum frae Gill Morice,
   It's deir welcum to mee.

Ze leid, ze leid, ze filthy nurse,
    Sae loud I heird zee lee;
I brocht it to Lord Barnards lady;
    I trow ze be nae shee.
Then up and spack the bauld baron,
    An angry man was hee;
He's tain the table wi' his foot,
    Sae has he wi' his knee;
Till siller cup and 'mazer' dish
    In flinders he gard flee.

Gae bring a robe of zour cliding,
    That hings upon the pin;
And I'll gae to the gude grene wode,
    And speik wi' zour lemman.
O bide at hame, now Lord Barnard,
    I warde ze bide at hame;
Neir wyte a man for violence,
    That neir wate ze wi' nane.

Gil Morice sate in gude grene wode,
    He whistled and he sang:
O what mean a' the folk coming,
    My mother tarries lang.
His hair was like the threeds of gold,
    Drawne frae Minerva's loome:
His lipps like roses drapping dew,
    His breath was a' perfume.

His brow was like the mountain snae
    Gilt by the morning beam:
His cheeks like living roses glow:

His een like azure stream.
The boy was clad in robes of grene,
   Sweete as the infant spring:
And like the mavis on the bush,
   He gart the vallies ring.

The baron came to the grene wode,
   Wi' mickle dule and care,
And there he first spied Gill Morice
   Kameing his zellow hair:
That sweetly wavd around his face,
   That face beyond compare:
He sang sae sweet it might dispel
   A' rage but fell despair.

Nae wonder, nae wonder, Gill Morice,
   My lady loed thee weel,
The fairest part of my bodie
   Is blacker than thy heel.
Zet neir the less now, Gill Morice,
   For a' thy great beautie,
Ze's rew the day ze eir was born;
   That head sall gae wi' me.

Now he has drawn his trusty brand,
   And slaited on the strae;
And thro' Gill Morice' fair body
   He's gar cauld iron gae.
And he has tain Gill Morice's head
   And set it on a speir;
The meanest man in a' his train
   Has gotten that head to bear.

And he has tain Gill Morice up,
    Laid him across his steid,
And brocht him to his painted bowr,
    And laid him on a bed.
The lady sat on castil wa',
    Beheld baith dale and doun;
And there she saw Gill Morice' head
    Cum trailing to the toun.

Far better I loe that bluidy head,
    Both and that zellow hair,
Than Lord Barnard, and a' his lands,
    As they lig here and thair.
And she has tain her Gill Morice,
    And kissd baith mouth and chin:
I was once as fow of Gill Morice,
    As the hip is o' the stean.

I got ze in my father's house,
    Wi' mickle sin and shame;
I brocht thee up in gude grene wode,
    Under the heavy rain.
Oft have I by thy cradle sitten,
    And fondly seen thee sleip;
But now I gae about thy grave,
    The saut tears for to weip.

And syne she kissd his bluidy cheik,
    And syne his bluidy chin:
O better I loe my Gill Morice
    Than a' my kith and kin!
Away, away, ze ill woman,

And an il deith mait ze dee:
Gin I had kend he'd bin zour son,
   He'd neir bin slain for mee.

Obraid me not, my Lord Barnard!
   Obraid me not for shame!
Wi' that saim speir O pierce my heart!
   And put me out o' pain.
Since nothing bot Gill Morice head
   Thy jelous rage could quell,
Let that saim hand now tak hir life,
   That neir to thee did ill.

To me nae after days nor nichts
   Will eir be saft or kind;
I'll fill the air with heavy sighs,
   And greet till I am blind.
Enouch of blood by me's been spilt,
   Seek not zour death frae mee;
I rather lourd it had been my sel
   Than eather him or thee.

With waefo wae I hear zour plaint;
   Sair, sair I rew the deid,
That eir this cursed hand of mine
   Had gard his body bleid.
Dry up zour tears, my winsome dame,
   Ze neir can heal the wound;
Ze see his head upon the speir,
   His heart's blude on the ground.

I curse the hand that did the deid,
  The heart that thocht the ill;
The feet that bore me wi' sik speid,
  The comely zouth to kill.
I'll ay lament for Gill Morice,
  As gin he were mine ain;
I'll neir forget the dreiry day
  On which the zouth was slain.

THE CHILD OF ELLE

On yondre hill a castle standes
　　With walles and towres bedight,
And yonder lives the Child of Elle,
　A younge and comely knighte.

The Child of Elle to his garden went,
　　And stood at his garden pale,
Whan, lo! he beheld fair Emmelines page
　　Come trippinge downe the dale.

The Child of Elle he hyed him thence,
　　Y-wis he stoode not stille,
And soone he mette faire Emmelines page
　　Come climbinge up the hille.

Nowe Christe thee save, thou little foot-page,
   Now Christe thee save and see!
Oh telle me how does thy ladye gaye,
   And what may thy tydinges bee?

My ladye shee is all woe-begone,
   And the teares they falle from her eyne;
And aye she laments the deadlye feude
   Betweene her house and thine.

And here shee sends thee a silken scarfe
   Bedewde with many a teare,
And biddes thee sometimes thinke on her,
   Who loved thee so deare.

And here shee sends thee a ring of golde
   The last boone thou mayst have,
And biddes thee weare it for her sake,
   Whan she is layde in grave.

For, ah! her gentle heart is broke,
   And in grave soone must shee bee,
Sith her father hath chose her a new new love,
   And forbidde her to think of thee.

Her father hath brought her a carlish knight,
   Sir John of the north countraye,
And within three dayes she must him wedde,
   Or he vowes he will her slaye.

Nowe hye thee backe, thou little foot-page,
   And greet thy ladye from mee,

And telle her that I her owne true love
    Will dye, or sette her free.

Nowe hye thee backe, thou little foot-page,
    And let thy fair ladye know
This night will I bee at her bowre-windowe,
    Betide me weale or woe.

The boye he tripped, the boye he ranne,
    He neither stint ne stayd
Untill he came to fair Emmelines bowre,
    Whan kneeling downe he sayd,

O ladye, I've been with thine own true love,
    And he greets thee well by mee;
This night will hee bee at thy bowre-windowe,
    And dye or sett thee free.

Nowe daye was gone, and night was come,
    And all were fast asleepe,
All save the Ladye Emmeline,
    Who sate in her bowre to weepe:

And soone shee heard her true loves voice
    Lowe whispering at the walle,
Awake, awake, my deare ladye,
    Tis I thy true love call.

Awake, awake, my ladye deare,
    Come, mount this faire palfraye:
This ladder of ropes will lette thee downe
    He carrye thee hence awaye.

Nowe nay, nowe nay, thou gentle knight,
    Nowe nay, this may not bee;
For aye shold I tint my maiden fame,
    If alone I should wend with thee.

O ladye, thou with a knighte so true
    Mayst safelye wend alone,
To my ladye mother I will thee bringe,
    Where marriage shall make us one.

"My father he is a baron bolde,
    Of lynage proude and hye;
And what would he saye if his daughter
    Awaye with a knight should fly

"Ah! well I wot, he never would rest,
    Nor his meate should doe him no goode,
Until he hath slayne thee, Child of Elle,
    And scene thy deare hearts bloode."

O ladye, wert thou in thy saddle sette,
    And a little space him fro,
I would not care for thy cruel father,
    Nor the worst that he could doe.

O ladye, wert thou in thy saddle sette,
    And once without this walle,
I would not care for thy cruel father
    Nor the worst that might befalle.

Faire Emmeline sighed, fair Emmeline wept,
    And aye her heart was woe:

At length he seized her lilly-white hand,
    And downe the ladder he drewe:

And thrice he clasped her to his breste,
    And kist her tenderlie:
The teares that fell from her fair eyes
    Ranne like the fountayne free.

Hee mounted himselfe on his steede so talle,
    And her on a fair palfraye,
And slung his bugle about his necke,
    And roundlye they rode awaye.

All this beheard her owne damselle,
    In her bed whereas shee ley,
Quoth shee, My lord shall knowe of this,
    Soe I shall have golde and fee.

Awake, awake, thou baron bolde!
    Awake, my noble dame!
Your daughter is fledde with the Child of Elle
    To doe the deede of shame.

The baron he woke, the baron he rose,
    And called his merrye men all:
"And come thou forth, Sir John the knighte,
    Thy ladye is carried to thrall."

Faire Emmeline scant had ridden a mile,
    A mile forth of the towne,
When she was aware of her fathers men
    Come galloping over the downe:

And foremost came the carlish knight,
   Sir John of the north countraye:
"Nowe stop, nowe stop, thou false traitoure,
   Nor carry that ladye awaye.

"For she is come of hye lineage,
   And was of a ladye borne,
And ill it beseems thee, a false churl's sonne,
   To carrye her hence to scorne."

Nowe loud thou lyest, Sir John the knight,
   Nowe thou doest lye of mee;
A knight mee gott, and a ladye me bore,
   Soe never did none by thee

But light nowe downe, my ladye faire,
   Light downe, and hold my steed,
While I and this discourteous knighte
   Doe trye this arduous deede.

But light now downe, my deare ladye,
   Light downe, and hold my horse;
While I and this discourteous knight
   Doe trye our valour's force.

Fair Emmeline sighed, fair Emmeline wept,
   And aye her heart was woe,
While twixt her love and the carlish knight
   Past many a baleful blowe.

The Child of Elle hee fought so well,
   As his weapon he waved amaine,

That soone he had slaine the carlish knight,
   And layd him upon the plaine.

And nowe the baron and all his men
   Full fast approached nye:
Ah! what may ladye Emmeline doe
   Twere nowe no boote to flye.

Her lover he put his horne to his mouth,
   And blew both loud and shrill,
And soone he saw his owne merry men
   Come ryding over the hill.

"Nowe hold thy hand, thou bold baron,
   I pray thee hold thy hand,
Nor ruthless rend two gentle hearts
   Fast knit in true love's band.

Thy daughter I have dearly loved
   Full long and many a day;
But with such love as holy kirke
   Hath freelye sayd wee may.

O give consent, shee may be mine,
   And blesse a faithfull paire:
My lands and livings are not small,
   My house and lineage faire:

My mother she was an earl's daughter,
   And a noble knyght my sire—
The baron he frowned, and turn'd away
   With mickle dole and ire.

Fair Emmeline sighed, faire Emmeline wept,
　　And did all tremblinge stand:
At lengthe she sprang upon her knee,
　　And held his lifted hand.

Pardon, my lorde and father deare,
　　This faire yong knyght and mee:
Trust me, but for the carlish knyght,
　　I never had fled from thee.

Oft have you called your Emmeline
　　Your darling and your joye;
O let not then your harsh resolves
　　Your Emmeline destroye.

The baron he stroakt his dark-brown cheeke,
　　And turned his heade asyde
To whipe away the starting teare
　　He proudly strave to hyde.

In deepe revolving thought he stoode,
　　And mused a little space;
Then raised faire Emmeline from the grounde,
　　With many a fond embrace.

Here take her, Child of Elle, he sayd,
　　And gave her lillye white hand;
Here take my deare and only child,
　　And with her half my land:

Thy father once mine honour wrongde
　　In dayes of youthful pride;

Do thou the injurye repayre
　　In fondnesse for thy bride.

And as thou love her, and hold her deare,
　　Heaven prosper thee and thine:
And nowe my blessing wend wi' thee,
　　My lovelye Emmeline.

CHILD WATERS

CHILD WATERS

Child Waters

Childe Waters in his stable stoode
   And stroakt his milke white steede:

To him a fayre yonge ladye came
    As ever ware womans weede.

Sayes, Christ you save, good Childe Waters;
    Sayes, Christ you save, and see:
My girdle of gold that was too longe,
    Is now too short for mee.

And all is with one chyld of yours,
    I feel sturre att my side:
My gowne of greene it is too straighte;
    Before, it was too wide.

If the child be mine, faire Ellen, he sayd,
    Be mine, as you tell mee;
Then take you Cheshire and Lancashire both,
    Take them your owne to bee.

If the childe be mine, fair Ellen, he sayd,
    Be mine, as you doe sweare;
Then take you Cheshire and Lancashire both,
    And make that child your heyre.

Shee saies, I had rather have one kisse,
    Child Waters, of thy mouth;
Than I wolde have Cheshire and Lancashire both,
    That laye by north and south.

And I had rather have one twinkling,
    Childe Waters, of thine ee;
Then I wolde have Cheshire and Lancashire both,
    To take them mine owne to bee.

To morrow, Ellen, I must forth ryde
    Farr into the north countrie;
The fairest lady that I can find,
    Ellen, must goe with mee.

'Thoughe I am not that lady fayre,
    'Yet let me go with thee:'
And ever I pray you, Child Waters,
    Your foot-page let me bee.

If you will my foot-page be, Ellen,
    As you doe tell to mee;
Then you must cut your gowne of greene,
    An inch above your knee:

Soe must you doe your yellow lockes,
    An inch above your ee:
You must tell no man what is my name;
    My foot-page then you shall bee.

Shee, all the long day Child Waters rode,
    Ran barefoote by his side;
Yett was he never soe courteous a knighte,
    To say, Ellen, will you ryde?

Shee, all the long day Child Waters rode,
    Ran barefoote thorow the broome;
Yett hee was never soe curteous a knighte,
    To say, put on your shoone.

Ride softlye, shee sayd, O Childe Waters,
    Why doe you ryde soe fast?

The childe, which is no mans but thine,
  My bodye itt will brast.

Hee sayth, seeth thou yonder water, Ellen,
  That flows from bank to brimme?—
I trust to God, O Child Waters,
  You never will see mee swimme.

But when shee came to the waters side,
  Shee sayled to the chinne:
Except the Lord of heaven be my speed,
  Now must I learne to swimme.

The salt waters bare up her clothes;
  Our Ladye bare upp her chinne:
Childe Waters was a woe man, good Lord,
  To see faire Ellen swimme.

And when shee over the water was,
  Shee then came to his knee:
He said, Come hither, thou fair Ellen,
  Loe yonder what I see.

Seest thou not yonder hall, Ellen?
  Of redd gold shines the yate;
Of twenty foure faire ladyes there,
  The fairest is my mate.

Seest thou not yonder hall, Ellen?
  Of redd gold shines the towre:
There are twenty four fair ladyes there,
  The fairest is my paramoure.

I see the hall now, Child Waters,
    Of redd golde shines the yate:
God give you good now of yourselfe,
    And of your worthye mate.

I see the hall now, Child Waters,
    Of redd gold shines the towre:
God give you good now of yourselfe,
    And of your paramoure.

There twenty four fayre ladyes were
    A playing att the ball:
And Ellen the fairest ladye there,
    Must bring his steed to the stall.

There twenty four fayre ladyes were
    A playinge at the chesse;
And Ellen the fayrest ladye there,
    Must bring his horse to gresse.

And then bespake Childe Waters sister,
    These were the wordes said shee:
You have the prettyest foot-page, brother,
    That ever I saw with mine ee.

But that his bellye it is soe bigg,
    His girdle goes wonderous hie:
And let him, I pray you, Childe Wateres,
    Goe into the chamber with mee.

It is not fit for a little foot-page,
    That has run throughe mosse and myre,

To go into the chamber with any ladye,
    That weares soe riche attyre.

It is more meete for a litle foot-page,
    That has run throughe mosse and myre,
To take his supper upon his knee,
    And sitt downe by the kitchen fyer.

But when they had supped every one,
    To bedd they tooke theyr waye:
He sayd, come hither, my little foot-page,
    And hearken what I saye.

Goe thee downe into yonder towne,
    And low into the street;
The fayrest ladye that thou can finde,

    Hyer her in mine armes to sleepe,
And take her up in thine armes twaine,
    For filinge of her feete.

Ellen is gone into the towne,
    And low into the streete:
The fairest ladye that she cold find,
    Shee hyred in his armes to sleepe;
And tooke her up in her armes twayne,
    For filing of her feete.

I pray you nowe, good Child Waters,
    Let mee lye at your bedds feete:
For there is noe place about this house,
    Where I may 'saye a sleepe.

'He gave her leave, and faire Ellen
    'Down at his beds feet laye:'
This done the nighte drove on apace,
    And when it was neare the daye,

Hee sayd, Rise up, my litle foot-page,
    Give my steede corne and haye;
And soe doe thou the good black oats,
    To carry mee better awaye.

Up then rose the faire Ellen,
    And gave his steede corne and hay:
And soe shee did the good blacke oats,
    To carry him the better away.

Shee leaned her backe to the manger side,
    And grievouslye did groane:
Shee leaned her backe to the manger side,
    And there shee made her moane.

And that beheard his mother deere,
    Shee heard her there monand.
Shee sayd, Rise up, thou Childe Waters,
    I think thee a cursed man.

For in thy stable is a ghost,
    That grievouslye doth grone:
Or else some woman laboures of childe,
    She is soe woe-begone.

Up then rose Childe Waters soon,
    And did on his shirte of silke;

And then he put on his other clothes,
    On his body as white as milke.

And when he came to the stable dore,
    Full still there he did stand,
That hee mighte heare his fayre Ellen
    Howe shee made her monand.

Shee sayd, Lullabye, mine owne deere child,
    Lullabye, dere child, dere;
I wold thy father were a king,
    Thy mother layd on a biere.

Peace now, he said, good faire Ellen,
    Be of good cheere, I praye;
And the bridal and the churching both
    Shall bee upon one day.

KING EDWARD IV &
THE TANNER OF TAMWORTH

King Edward IV & the
Tanner of Tamworth

In summer time, when leaves grow greene,
   And blossoms bedecke the tree,
King Edward wolde a hunting ryde,
   Some pastime for to see.

With hawke and hounde he made him bowne,
   With horne, and eke with bowe;
To Drayton Basset he tooke his waye,
   With all his lordes a rowe.

And he had ridden ore dale and downe
   By eight of clocke in the day,

When he was ware of a bold tanner,
    Come ryding along the waye.

A fayre russet coat the tanner had on
    Fast buttoned under his chin,
And under him a good cow-hide,
    And a marc of four shilling.

Nowe stand you still, my good lordes all,
    Under the grene wood spraye;
And I will wend to yonder fellowe,
    To weet what he will saye.

God speede, God speede thee, said our king.
    Thou art welcome, Sir, sayd hee.
"The readyest waye to Drayton Basset
    I praye thee to shew to mee."

"To Drayton Basset woldst thou goe,
    Fro the place where thou dost stand?
The next payre of gallowes thou comest unto,
    Turne in upon thy right hand."

That is an unreadye waye, sayd our king,
    Thou doest but jest, I see;
Nowe shewe me out the nearest waye,
    And I pray thee wend with mee.

Away with a vengeance! quoth the tanner:
    I hold thee out of thy witt:
All daye have I rydden on Brocke my mare,
    And I am fasting yett.

"Go with me downe to Drayton Basset,
    No daynties we will spare;
All daye shalt thou eate and drinke of the best,
    And I will paye thy fare."

Gramercye for nothing, the tanner replyde,
    Thou payest no fare of mine:
I trowe I've more nobles in my purse,
    Than thou hast pence in thine.

God give thee joy of them, sayd the king,
    And send them well to priefe.
The tanner wolde faine have beene away,
    For he weende he had beene a thiefe.

What art thou, hee sayde, thou fine fellowe,
    Of thee I am in great feare,
For the clothes, thou wearest upon thy back,
    Might beseeme a lord to weare.

I never stole them, quoth our king,
    I tell you, Sir, by the roode.
"Then thou playest, as many an unthrift doth,
    And standest in midds of thy goode."

What tydinges heare you, sayd the kynge,
    As you ryde farre and neare?
"I heare no tydinges, Sir, by the masse,
    But that cowe-hides are deare."

"Cow-hides! cow-hides! what things are those?
    I marvell what they bee?"

What, art thou a foole? the tanner reply'd;
    I carry one under mee.

What craftsman art thou, said the king,
    I pray thee tell me trowe.
"I am a barker, Sir, by my trade;
    Nowe tell me what art thou?"

I am a poor courtier, Sir, quoth he,
    That am forth of service worne;
And faine I wolde thy prentise bee,
    Thy cunninge for to learne.

Marrye heaven forfend, the tanner replyde,
    That thou my prentise were:
Thou woldst spend more good than I shold winne
    By fortye shilling a yere.

Yet one thinge wolde I, sayd our king,
    If thou wilt not seeme strange:
Thoughe my horse be better than thy mare,
    Yet with thee I fain wold change.

"Why if with me thou faine wilt change,
    As change full well maye wee,
By the faith of my bodye, thou proude fellowe
    I will have some boot of thee."

That were against reason, sayd the king,
    I sweare, so mote I thee:
My horse is better than thy mare,
    And that thou well mayst see.

"Yea, Sir, but Brocke is gentle and mild,
　　And softly she will fare:
Thy horse is unrulye and wild, I wiss;
　　Aye skipping here and theare."

What boote wilt thou have? our king reply'd;
　　Now tell me in this stound.
"Noe pence, nor halfpence, by my faye,
　　But a noble in gold so round.

"Here's twentye groates of white moneye,
　　Sith thou will have it of mee."
I would have sworne now, quoth the tanner,
　　Thou hadst not had one pennie.

But since we two have made a change,
　　A change we must abide,
Although thou hast gotten Brocke my mare,
　　Thou gettest not my cowe-hide.

I will not have it, sayd the kynge,
　　I sweare, so mought I thee;
Thy foule cowe-hide I wolde not beare,
　　If thou woldst give it to mee.

The tanner hee tooke his good cowe-hide,
　　That of the cow was bilt;
And threwe it upon the king's sadelle,
　　That was soe fayrelye gilte.
"Now help me up, thou fine fellowe,
　　'Tis time that I were gone:

When I come home to Gyllian my wife,
    Sheel say I am a gentilmon."

The king he tooke him up by the legge;
    The tanner a f—lett fall.
Nowe marrye, good fellowe, sayd the king,
    Thy courtesye is but small.

When the tanner he was in the kinges sadelle,
    And his foote in the stirrup was;
He marvelled greatlye in his minde,
    Whether it were golde or brass.

But when the steede saw the cows taile wagge,
    And eke the blacke cowe-horne;
He stamped, and stared, and awaye he ranne,
    As the devill had him borne.

The tanner he pulld, the tanner he sweat,
    And held by the pummil fast:
At length the tanner came tumbling downe;
    His necke he had well-nye brast.

Take thy horse again with a vengeance, he sayd,
    With mee he shall not byde.
"My horse wolde have borne thee well enoughe,
    But he knewe not of thy cowe-hide.

Yet if againe thou faine woldst change,
    As change full well may wee,
By the faith of my bodye, thou jolly tanner,
    I will have some boote of thee."

What boote wilt thou have? the tanner replyd,
 Nowe tell me in this stounde.
"Noe pence nor halfpence, Sir, by my faye,
 But I will have twentye pound."

"Here's twentye groates out of my purse;
 And twentye I have of thine:
And I have one more, which we will spend
 Together at the wine."

The king set a bugle home to his mouthe,
 And blewe both loude and shrille:
And soone came lords, and soone came knights,
 Fast ryding over the hille.

Nowe, out alas! the tanner he cryde,
 That ever I sawe this daye!
Thou art a strong thiefe, yon come thy fellowes
 Will beare my cowe-hide away.

They are no thieves, the king replyde,
 I sweare, soe mote I thee:
But they are the lords of the north countrey,
 Here come to hunt with mee.

And soone before our king they came,
 And knelt downe on the grounde:
Then might the tanner have beene awaye,
 He had lever than twentye pounde.

A coller, a coller, here: sayd the king,
 A coller he loud gan crye:

Then woulde he lever than twentye pound,
   He had not beene so nighe.

A coller, a coller, the tanner he sayd,
   I trowe it will breed sorrowe:
After a coller cometh a halter,
   I trow I shall be hang'd to-morrowe.

Be not afraid, tanner, said our king;
   I tell thee, so mought I thee,
Lo here I make thee the best esquire
   That is in the North countrie.

For Plumpton-parke I will give thee,
   With tenements faire beside:
'Tis worth three hundred markes by the yeare,
   To maintaine thy good cowe-hide.

Gramercye, my liege, the tanner replyde,
   For the favour thou hast me showne;
If ever thou comest to merry Tamworth,
   Neates leather shall clout thy shoen.

SIR PATRICK SPENS

SIR PATRICK SPENS

The king sits in Dumferling toune,
    Drinking the blude-reid wine:
O quhar will I get guid sailor,
    To sail this schip of mine.

Up and spak an eldern knicht,
    Sat at the kings richt kne:
Sir Patrick Spens is the best sailor,
    That sails upon the se.

The king has written a braid letter,
    And signd it wi' his hand;
And sent it to Sir Patrick Spens,
    Was walking on the sand.

The first line that Sir Patrick red,
    A loud lauch lauched he:

The next line that Sir Patrick red,
  The teir blinded his ee.

O quha is this has don this deid,
  This ill deid don to me;
To send me out this time o' the zeir,
  To sail upon the se.

Mak hast, mak haste, my mirry men all,
  Our guid schip sails the morne,
O say na sae, my master deir,
  For I feir a deadlie storme.

Late late yestreen I saw the new moone
  Wi' the auld moone in hir arme;
And I feir, I feir, my deir master,
  That we will com to harme.

O our Scots nobles wer richt laith
  To weet their cork-heild schoone;
Bot lang owre a' the play wer playd,
  Thair hats they swam aboone.

O lang, lang, may thair ladies sit
  Wi' thair fans into their hand,
Or eir they se Sir Patrick Spens
  Cum sailing to the land.

O lang, lang, may the ladies stand
  Wi' thair gold kems in their hair,
Waiting for thair ain deir lords,
  For they'll se thame na mair.

Have owre, have owre to Aberdour,
   It's fiftie fadom deip:
And thair lies guid Sir Patrick Spens,
   Wi' the Scots lords at his feit.

THE EARL OF MAR'S DAUGHTER

It was intill a pleasant time,
    Upon a simmer's day,
The noble Earl of Mar's daughter
    Went forth to sport and play.

As thus she did amuse hersell,
    Below a green aik tree,
There she saw a sprightly doo
    Set on a tower sae hie.

"O cow-me-doo, my love sae true,
    If ye'll come down to me,
Ye 'se hae a cage o guid red gowd
    Instead o simple tree:

"I'll put growd hingers roun your cage,
    And siller roun your wa;
I'll gar ye shine as fair a bird
    As ony o them a'."

But she hadnae these words well spoke,
    Nor yet these words well said,
Till Cow-me-doo flew frae the tower
    And lighted on her head.

Then she has brought this pretty bird
    Hame to her bowers and ba,
And made him shine as fair a bird
    As ony o them a'.

When day was gane, and night was come,
    About the evening tide,
This lady spied a sprightly youth
    Stand straight up by her side.

"From whence came ye, young man?" she said;
    "That does surprise me sair;
My door was bolted right secure,
    What way hae ye come here?"

"O had your tongue, ye lady fair,
    Lat a' your folly be;
Mind ye not on your turtle-doo
    Last day ye brought wi thee?"

"O tell me mair, young man," she said,
    "This does surprise me now;

What country hae ye come frae?
    What pedigree are you?"

"My mither lives on foreign isles,
    She has nae mair but me;
She is a queen o wealth and state,
    And birth and high degree.

"Likewise well skilld in magic spells,
    As ye may plainly see,
And she transformd me to yon shape,
    To charm such maids as thee.

"I am a doo the live-lang day,
    A sprightly youth at night;
This aye gars me appear mair fair
    In a fair maiden's sight.

"And it was but this verra day
    That I came ower the sea;
Your lovely face did me enchant;
    I'll live and dee wi thee."

"O Cow-me-doo, my luve sae true,
    Nae mair frae me ye 'se gae;
That's never my intent, my luve,
    As ye said, it shall be sae."

"O Cow-me-doo, my luve sae true,
    It's time to gae to bed;"
"Wi a' my heart, my dear marrow,
    It's be as ye hae said."

Then he has staid in bower wi her
    For sax lang years and ane,
Till sax young sons to him she bare,
    And the seventh she's brought hame.

But aye as ever a child was born
    He carried them away,
And brought them to his mither's care,
    As fast as he coud fly.

Thus he has staid in bower wi her
    For twenty years and three;
There came a lord o high renown
    To court this fair ladie.

But still his proffer she refused,
    And a' his presents too;
Says, I'm content to live alane
    Wi my bird, Cow-me-doo.

Her father sware a solemn oath
    Amang the nobles all,
"The morn, or ere I eat or drink,
    This bird I will gar kill."

The bird was sitting in his cage,
    And heard what they did say;
And when he found they were dismist,
    Says, Wae's me for this day!

"Before that I do langer stay,
    And thus to be forlorn,

I'll gang unto my mither's bower,
   Where I was bred and born."

Then Cow-me-doo took flight and flew
   Beyond the raging sea,
And lighted near his mither's castle,
   On a tower o gowd sae hie.

As his mither was wauking out,
   To see what she coud see,
And there she saw her little son,
   Set on the tower sae hie.

"Get dancers here to dance," she said,
   "And minstrells for to play;
For here's my young son, Florentine,
   Come here wi me to stay."

"Get nae dancers to dance, mither,
   Nor minstrells for to play,
For the mither o my seven sons,
   The morn's her wedding-day."

"O tell me, tell me, Florentine,
   Tell me, and tell me true,
Tell me this day without a flaw,
   What I will do for you."

"Instead of dancers to dance, mither,
   Or minstrells for to play,
Turn four-and-twenty wall-wight men
   Like storks in feathers gray;

"My seven sons in seven swans,
 Aboon their heads to flee;
And I mysell a gay gos-hawk,
 A bird o high degree."

Then sichin said the queen hersell,
 "That thing's too high for me;"
But she applied to an auld woman,
 Who had mair skill than she.

Instead o dancers to dance a dance,
 Or minstrells for to play,
Four-and-twenty wall-wight men
 Turnd birds o feathers gray;

Her seven sons in seven swans,
 Aboon their heads to flee;
And he himsell a gay gos-hawk,
 A bird o high degree.

This flock o birds took flight and flew
 Beyond the raging sea,
And landed near the Earl Mar's castle,
 Took shelter in every tree.

They were a flock o pretty birds,
 Right comely to be seen;
The people viewed them wi surprise,
 As they dancd on the green.

These birds ascended frae the tree
 And lighted on the ha,

And at the last wi force did flee
    Amang the nobles a'.

The storks there seized some o the men,
    They coud neither fight nor flee;
The swans they bound the bride's best man
    Below a green aik tree.

They lighted next on maidens fair,
    Then on the bride's own head,
And wi the twinkling o an ee
    The bride and them were fled.

There's ancient men at weddings been
    For sixty years or more,
But sic a curious wedding-day
    They never saw before.

For naething coud the companie do.
    Nor naething coud they say
But they saw a flock o pretty birds
    That took their bride away.

When that Earl Mar he came to know
    Where his dochter did stay,
He signd a bond o unity,
    And visits now they pay.

EDWARD, EDWARD.

Quhy dois zour brand sae drop wi' bluid,
       Edward, Edward?
Quhy dois zour brand sae drop wi' bluid?
  And quhy sae sad gang zee, O?
O, I hae killed my hauke sae guid,
       Mither, mither:
O, I hae killed my hauke sae guid:
    And I had nae mair bot hee, O.

Zour haukis bluid was nevir sae reid,
       Edward, Edward.
Zour haukis bluid was nevir sae reid,
    My deir son I tell thee, O.

O, I hae killed my reid-roan steid,
      Mither, mither:
O, I hae killed my reid-roan steid,
       That erst was sae fair and free, O.

Zour steid was auld, and ze hae gat mair,
      Edward, Edward;
Zour steid was auld, and ze hae gat mair,
      Sum other dule ze drie, O.
O, I hae killed my fadir deir,
      Mither, mither:
O, I hae killed my fadir deir,
      Alas! and wae is mee, O!

And quhatten penance wul ze drie for that,
      Edward, Edward?
And quhatten penance will ze drie for that?
      My deir son, now tell mee, O.
He set my feit in zonder boat,
      Mither, mither:
He set my feit in zonder boat,
      And He fare ovir the sea, O.

And quhat wul ze doe wi' zour towirs and zour ha',
      Edward, Edward?
And quhat wul ze doe wi' zour towirs and zour ha',
      That were sae fair to see, O?
He let thame stand til they doun fa',
      Mither, mither:
He let thame stand til they doun fa',
      For here nevir mair maun I bee, O.

And quhat wul ze leive to zour bairns and zour wife,
Edward, Edward?
And quhat wul ze leive to zour bairns and zour wife,
Quhan ze gang ovir the sea, O?
The warldis room, let thame beg throw life,
Mither, mither;
The warldis room, let thame beg throw life,
For thame nevir mair wul I see, O.

And quhat wul ze leive to zour ain mither deir,
Edward, Edward?
And quhat wul ze leive to zour ain mither deir?
My deir son, now tell me, O.
The curse of hell frae me sail ze beir,
Mither, mither:
The curse of hell frae me sail ze beir,
Sic counseils ze gave to me, O.

KING LEIR & HIS THREE DAUGHTERS

King Leir once ruled in this land
   With princely power and peace;
And had all things with hearts content,
   That might his joys increase.
Amongst those things that nature gave,
   Three daughters fair had he,
So princely seeming beautiful,
   As fairer could not be.

So on a time it pleas'd the king
   A question thus to move,
Which of his daughters to his grace
   Could shew the dearest love:

For to my age you bring content,
    Quoth he, then let me hear,
Which of you three in plighted troth
    The kindest will appear.

To whom the eldest thus began;
    Dear father, mind, quoth she,
Before your face, to do you good,
    My blood shall render'd be:
And for your sake my bleeding heart
    Shall here be cut in twain,
Ere that I see your reverend age
    The smallest grief sustain.

And so will I, the second said;
    Dear father, for your sake,
The worst of all extremities
    I'll gently undertake:
And serve your highness night and day
    With diligence and love;
That sweet content and quietness
    Discomforts may remove.

In doing so, you glad my soul,
    The aged king reply'd;
But what sayst thou, my youngest girl,
    How is thy love ally'd?
My love (quoth young Cordelia then)
    Which to your grace I owe,
Shall be the duty of a child,
    And that is all I'll show.

And wilt thou shew no more, quoth he,
    Than doth thy duty bind?
I well perceive thy love is small,
    When as no more I find.
Henceforth I banish thee my court,
    Thou art no child of mine;
Nor any part of this my realm
    By favour shall be thine.

Thy elder sisters loves are more
    Then well I can demand,
To whom I equally bestow
    My kingdome and my land,
My pompal state and all my goods,
    That lovingly I may
With those thy sisters be maintain'd
    Until my dying day.

Thus flattering speeches won renown,
    By these two sisters here;
The third had causeless banishment,
    Yet was her love more dear:
For poor Cordelia patiently
    Went wandring up and down,
Unhelp'd, unpity'd, gentle maid,
    Through many an English town:

Untill at last in famous France
    She gentler fortunes found;
Though poor and bare, yet she was deem'd
    The fairest on the ground:
Where when the king her virtues heard,

And this fair lady seen,
With full consent of all his court
    He made his wife and queen.

Her father king Leir this while
    With his two daughters staid:
Forgetful of their promis'd loves,
    Full soon the same decay'd;
And living in queen Ragan's court,
    The eldest of the twain,
She took from him his chiefest means,
    And most of all his train.

For whereas twenty men were wont
    To wait with bended knee:
She gave allowance but to ten,
    And after scarce to three;
Nay, one she thought too much for him;
    So took she all away,
In hope that in her court, good king,
    He would no longer stay.

Am I rewarded thus, quoth he,
    In giving all I have
Unto my children, and to beg
    For what I lately gave?
I'll go unto my Gonorell:
    My second child, I know,
Will be more kind and pitiful,
    And will relieve my woe.

Full fast he hies then to her court;
   Where when she heard his moan
Return'd him answer, That she griev'd
   That all his means were gone:
But no way could relieve his wants;
   Yet if that he would stay
Within her kitchen, he should have
   What scullions gave away.

When he had heard, with bitter tears,
   He made his answer then;
In what I did let me be made
   Example to all men.
I will return again, quoth he,
   Unto my Ragan's court;
She will not use me thus, I hope,
   But in a kinder sort.

Where when he came, she gave command
   To drive him thence away:
When he was well within her court
   (She said) he would not stay.
Then back again to Gonorell
   The woeful king did hie,
That in her kitchen he might have
   What scullion boy set by.

But there of that he was deny'd,
   Which she had promis'd late:
For once refusing, he should not
   Come after to her gate.
Thus twixt his daughters, for relief

He wandred up and down;
Being glad to feed on beggars food,
   That lately wore a crown.

And calling to remembrance then
   His youngest daughters words,
That said the duty of a child
   Was all that love affords:
But doubting to repair to her,
   Whom he had banish'd so,
Grew frantick mad; for in his mind
   He bore the wounds of woe:

Which made him rend his milk-white locks,
   And tresses from his head,
And all with blood bestain his cheeks,
   With age and honour spread.
To hills and woods and watry founts
   He made his hourly moan,
Till hills and woods and sensless things,
   Did seem to sigh and groan.

Even thus possest with discontents,
   He passed o're to France,
In hopes from fair Cordelia there,
   To find some gentler chance;
Most virtuous dame! which when she heard,
   Of this her father's grief,
As duty bound, she quickly sent
   Him comfort and relief:
And by a train of noble peers,
   In brave and gallant sort,

She gave in charge he should be brought
    To Aganippus' court;
Whose royal king, with noble mind
    So freely gave consent,
To muster up his knights at arms,
    To fame and courage bent.

And so to England came with speed,
    To repossesse king Leir
And drive his daughters from their thrones
    By his Cordelia dear.
Where she, true-hearted noble queen,
    Was in the battel slain;
Yet he, good king, in his old days,
    Possest his crown again.

But when he heard Cordelia's death,
    Who died indeed for love
Of her dear father, in whose cause
    She did this battle move;
He swooning fell upon her breast,
    From whence he never parted:
But on her bosom left his life,
    That was so truly hearted.

The lords and nobles when they saw
    The end of these events,
The other sisters unto death
    They doomed by consents;
And being dead, their crowns they left
    Unto the next of kin:
Thus have you seen the fall of pride,
    And disobedient sin.

HYND HORN

"Hynde Horn's bound, love, and Hynde Horn's free;
Whare was ye born? or frae what cuntrie?"

"In gude greenwud whare I was born,
And all my friends left me forlorn.

"I gave my love a gay gowd wand,
That was to rule oure all Scotland.

"My love gave me a silver ring,
That was to rule abune aw thing.

"Whan that ring keeps new in hue,
Ye may ken that your love loves you.

"Whan that ring turns pale and wan,
Ye may ken that your love loves anither man."

He hoisted up his sails, and away sailed he
Till he cam to a foreign cuntree.

Whan he lookit to his ring, it was turnd pale and wan;
Says, I wish I war at hame again.

He hoisted up his sails, and hame sailed he
Until he cam till his ain cuntree.

The first ane that he met with,
It was with a puir auld beggar-man.

"What news? what news, my puir auld man?
What news hae ye got to tell to me?"

"Na news, na news," the puir man did say,
"But this is our queen's wedding-day."

"Ye'll lend me your begging-weed,
And I'll lend you my riding-steed."

"My begging-weed is na for thee,
Your riding-steed is na for me."

He has changed wi the puir auld beggar-man.

"What is the way that ye use to gae?
And what are the words that ye beg wi?"

"Whan ye come to yon high hill,
Ye'll draw your bent bow nigh until.

"Whan ye come to yon town-end,
Ye'll lat your bent bow low fall doun.

"Ye'll seek meat for St Peter, ask for St Paul,
And seek for the sake of your Hynde Horn all.

"But tak ye frae nane o them aw
Till ye get frae the bonnie bride hersel O."

Whan he cam to yon high hill,
He drew his bent bow nigh until.

And when he cam to yon toun-end,
He loot his bent bow low fall doun.

He sought for St Peter, he askd for St Paul,
And he sought for the sake of his Hynde Horn all.

But he took na frae ane o them aw
Till he got frae the bonnie bride hersel O.

The bride cam tripping doun the stair,
Wi the scales o red gowd on her hair.

Wi a glass o red wine in her hand,
To gie to the puir beggar-man.

Out he drank his glass o wine,
Into it he dropt the ring.

"Got ye't by sea, or got ye't by land,
Or got ye't aff a drownd man's hand?"

"I got na't by sea, I got na't by land,
Nor gat I it aff a drownd man's hand;

"But I got it at my wooing,
And I'll gie it to your wedding."

"I'll tak the scales o gowd frae my head,
I'll follow you, and beg my bread.

"I'll tak the scales o gowd frae my hair,
I'll follow you for evermair."

She has tane the scales o gowd frae her head,
She's followed him, to beg her bread.

She has tane the scales o gowd frae her hair,
And she has followd him evermair.

Atween the kitchen and the ha,
There he loot his cloutie cloak fa.

The red gowd shined oure them aw,
And the bride frae the bridegroom was stown awa.

JOHN BROWN'S BODY

Old John Brown's body lies a mould'ring in the grave,
Because he fought for Freedom and the stricken Negro slave;
Old John Brown's body lies a mould'ring in the grave,
But his soul is marching on.

Chorus

    Glory, glory, Hallelujah!
    Glory, glory, Hallelujah!
    Glory, glory, Hallelujah!
    His soul is marching on.

He was a noble martyr, was Old John Brown the true;
His little patriot band into a noble army grew;
He was a noble martyr, was Old John Brown the true,
And his soul is marching on.

253

'Twas not till John Brown lost his life, arose in all its might,
The army of the Union men that won the fearful fight;
But tho' the glad event, oh! it never met his sight,
Still his soul is marching on.

John Brown is now a soldier in that heavenly land above,
Where live the happy spirits in their harmony and love,
John Brown is now a soldier in that heavenly land above,
And his soul is marching on.

TIPPERARY

Up to mighty London came an Irishman one day,
As the streets are paved with gold, sure everyone was gay;
Singing songs of Piccadilly, Strand and Leicester Square,
Till Paddy got excited, then he shouted to them there:—

Chorus

"It's a long way to Tipperary,
It's a long way to go;
It's a long way to Tipperary,
To the sweetest girl I know!
Good-bye Piccadilly,
Farewell, Leicester Square,
It's a long, long way to Tipperary,
But my heart's right there!"

Paddy wrote a letter to his Irish Molly O',
Saying, "Should you not receive it, write and let me know!
"If I make mistakes in 'spelling,' Molly dear,' said he,
"Remember it's the pen that's bad, don't lay the blame on me."

Molly wrote a neat reply to Irish Paddy O',
Saying, "Mike Maloney wants to marry me, and so
Leave the Strand and Piccadilly, or you'll be to blame,
For love has fairly drove me silly—hoping you're the same!"

THE BAILIFF'S DAUGHTER OF ISLINGTON

The Bailiff's Daughter of Islington

There was a youthe, and a well-beloved youthe,
    And he was a squires son:
He loved the bayliffes daughter deare,
    That lived in Islington.

Yet she was coye, and would not believe
    That he did love her soe,
Noe nor at any time would she
    Any countenance to him showe.

But when his friendes did understand
    His fond and foolish minde,
They sent him up to faire London
    An apprentice for to binde.

And when he had been seven long yeares,
    And never his love could see:
Many a teare have I shed for her sake,
    When she little thought of mee.

Then all the maids of Islington
    Went forth to sport and playe,
All but the bayliffes daughter deare;
    She secretly stole awaye.

She pulled off her gowne of greene,
    And put on ragged attire,
And to faire London she would goe
    Her true love to enquire.

And as she went along the high road,
    The weather being hot and drye,
She sat her downe upon a green bank,
    And her true love came riding bye.

She started up, with a colour soe redd,
    Catching hold of his bridle-reine;

One penny, one penny, kind Sir, she sayd,
   Will ease me of much paine.

Before I give you one penny, sweet-heart,
   Praye tell me where you were borne:
At Islington, kind Sir, sayd shee,
   Where I have had many a scorne.

I prythee, sweet-heart, then tell to mee,
   O tell me, whether you knowe
The bayliffes daughter of Islington:
   She is dead, Sir, long agoe.

If she be dead, then take my horse,
   My saddle and bridle also;
For I will into some far countrye,
   Where noe man shall me knowe.

O staye, O staye, thou goodlye youthe,
   She standeth by thy side;
She is here alive, she is not dead,
   And readye to be thy bride.

O farewell griefe, and welcome joye,
   Ten thousand times therefore;
For nowe I have founde mine owne true love,
   Whom I thought I should never see more.

THE THREE RAVENS

There were three rauens sat on a tree,
   Downe a downe, hay down, hay downe
There were three rauens sat on a tree,

With a downe
There were three rauens sat on a tree,
They were as blacke as they might be
    With a downe derrie, derrie, derrie, downe, downe

The one of them said to his mate,
"Where shall we our breakefast take?"

"Downe in yonder greene field,
There lies a knight slain vnder his shield.

"His hounds they lie downe at his feete,
So well they can their master keepe.

"His haukes they flie so eagerly,
There's no fowle dare him come nie."

Downe there comes a fallow doe,
As great with yong as she might goe.

She lift up his bloudy hed,
And kist his wounds that were so red.

She got him up upon her backe,
And carried him to earthen lake.

She buried him before the prime,
She was dead herselfe ere even-song time.

God send every gentleman,
Such haukes, such hounds, and such a leman.

THE GABERLUNZIE MAN

The pauky auld Carle come ovir the lee
Wi' mony good-eens and days to mee,
Saying, Good wife, for zour courtesie,
    Will ze lodge a silly poor man?
The night was cauld, the carle was wat,
And down azont the ingle he sat;
My dochtors shoulders he gan to clap,
    And cadgily ranted and sang.

O wow! quo he, were I as free,
As first when I saw this countrie,
How blyth and merry wad I bee!
    And I wad nevir think lang.
He grew canty, and she grew fain;

But little did her auld minny ken
What thir slee twa togither were say'n,
  When wooing they were sa thrang.

And O! quo he, ann ze were as black,
As evir the crown of your dadyes hat,
Tis I wad lay thee by my backe,
  And awa wi' me thou sould gang.
And O! quoth she, ann I were as white,
As evir the snaw lay on the dike,
Ild dead me braw, and lady-like,
  And awa with thee Ild gang.

Between them twa was made a plot;
They raise a wee before the cock,
And wyliely they shot the lock,
  And fast to the bent are they gane.
Up the morn the auld wife raise,
And at her leisure put on her claiths,
Syne to the servants bed she gaes
  To speir for the silly poor man.

She gaed to the bed, whair the beggar lay,
The strae was cauld, he was away,
She clapt her hands, cryd, Dulefu' day!
  For some of our geir will be gane.
Some ran to coffer, and some to kist,
But nought was stown that could be mist.
She dancid her lane, cryd, Praise be blest,
  I have lodgd a leal poor man.

Since naithings awa, as we can learn,
The kirns to kirn, and milk to earn,
Gae butt the house, lass, and waken my bairn,
    And bid her come quickly ben.
The servant gaed where the dochter lay,
The sheets was cauld, she was away,
And fast to her goodwife can say,
    Shes aff with the gaberlunzie-man.

O fy gar ride, and fy gar rin,
And haste ze, find these traitors agen;
For shees be burnt, and hees be slein,
    The wearyfou gaberlunzie-man.
Some rade upo horse, some ran a fit
The wife was wood, and out o' her wit;
She could na gang, nor yet could sit,
    But ay did curse and did ban.

Mean time far hind out owre the lee,
For snug in a glen, where nane could see,
The twa, with kindlie sport and glee
    Cut frae a new cheese a whang.
The priving was gude, it pleas'd them baith,
To lo'e her for ay, he gae her his aith.
Quo she, to leave thee, I will laith,
    My winsome gaberlunzie-man.

O kend my minny I were wi' zou,
Illfardly wad she crook her mou,
Sic a poor man sheld nevir trow,
    Aftir the gaberlunzie-mon.
My dear, quo he, zee're zet owre zonge;

264

And hae na learnt the beggars tonge,
To follow me frae toun to toun,
 And carrie the gaberlunzie on.

Wi' kauk and keel, Ill win zour bread,
And spindles and whorles for them wha need,
Whilk is a gentil trade indeed
 The gaberlunzie to carrie—o.
Ill bow my leg and crook my knee,
And draw a black clout owre my ee,
A criple or blind they will cau me:
 While we sail sing and be merrie—o.

THE WIFE OF USHER'S WELL

There lived a wife at Usher's Well,
    And a wealthy wife was she;
She had three stout and stalwart sons,
    And sent them oer the sea.

They hadna been a week from her,
    A week but barely ane,
Whan word came to the carline wife
    That her three sons were gane.

They hadna been a week from her,
    A week but barely three,
Whan word came to the carlin wife
    That her sons she'd never see.

"I wish the wind may never cease,
    Nor fashes in the flood,
Till my three sons come hame to me,
    In earthly flesh and blood."

It fell about the Martinmass,
    When nights are lang and mirk,
The carlin wife's three sons came hame,
    And their hats were o the birk.

It neither grew in syke nor ditch,
    Nor yet in ony sheugh;
But at the gates o Paradise,
    That birk grew fair eneugh.

* * * * *

"Blow up the fire, my maidens,
    Bring water from the well;
For a' my house shall feast this night,
    Since my three sons are well."

And she has made to them a bed,
    She's made it large and wide,
And she's taen her mantle her about,
    Sat down at the bed-side.

　　　　* * * * *

Up then crew the red, red cock,
    And up and crew the gray;
The eldest to the youngest said,
'Tis time we were away.

The cock he hadna crawd but once,
    And clappd his wings at a',
When the youngest to the eldest said,
    Brother, we must awa.

"The cock doth craw, the day doth daw,
    The channerin worm doth chide;
Gin we be mist out o our place,
    A sair pain we maun bide.

"Fare ye weel, my mother dear!
   Fareweel to barn and byre!
And fare ye weel, the bonny lass
   That kindles my mother's fire!"

THE LYE

Goe, soule, the bodies guest,
   Upon a thanklesse arrant;
Feare not to touche the best,
   The truth shall be thy warrant:
      Goe, since I needs must dye,
      And give the world the lye.

Goe tell the court, it glowes
   And shines like rotten wood;
Goe tell the church it showes
   What's good, and doth no good:
      If church and court reply,
      Then give them both the lye.

Tell potentates they live
　　Acting by others actions;
Not lov'd unlesse they give,
　　Not strong but by their factions;
　　　　If potentates reply,
　　　　Give potentates the lye.

Tell men of high condition,
　　That rule affairs of state,
Their purpose is ambition,
　　Their practise onely hate;
　　　　And if they once reply,
　　　　Then give them all the lye.

Tell them that brave it most,
　　They beg for more by spending,
Who in their greatest cost
　　Seek nothing but commending;
　　　　And if they make reply,
　　　　Spare not to give the lye.

Tell zeale, it lacks devotion;
　　Tell love, it is but lust;
Tell time, it is but motion;
　　Tell flesh, it is but dust;
　　　　And wish them not reply,
　　　　For thou must give the lye.

Tell age, it daily wasteth;
　　Tell honour, how it alters:
Tell beauty, how she blasteth;
　　Tell favour, how she falters;

And as they shall reply,
Give each of them the lye.

Tell wit, how much it wrangles
    In tickle points of nicenesse;
Tell wisedome, she entangles
    Herselfe in over-wisenesse;
            And if they do reply,
            Straight give them both the lye.

Tell physicke of her boldnesse;
    Tell skill, it is pretension;
Tell charity of coldness;
    Tell law, it is contention;
            And as they yield reply,
            So give them still the lye.

Tell fortune of her blindnesse;
    Tell nature of decay;
Tell friendship of unkindnesse;
    Tell justice of delay:
            And if they dare reply,
            Then give them all the lye.

Tell arts, they have no soundnesse,
    But vary by esteeming;
Tell schooles, they want profoundnesse;
    And stand too much on seeming:
            If arts and schooles reply.
            Give arts and schooles the lye.

Tell faith, it's fled the citie;
  Tell how the countrey erreth;
Tell, manhood shakes off pitie;
  Tell, vertue least preferreth:
        And, if they doe reply,
        Spare not to give the lye.

So, when thou hast, as I
  Commanded thee, done blabbing,
Although to give the lye
  Deserves no less than stabbing,
        Yet stab at thee who will,
        No stab the soule can kill.

THE BALLAD OF READING GAOL

I.

He did not wear his scarlet coat,
   For blood and wine are red,
And blood and wine were on his hands
   When they found him with the dead,
The poor dead woman whom he loved,
   And murdered in her bed.

He walked amongst the Trial Men
   In a suit of shabby grey;
A cricket cap was on his head,
   And his step seemed light and gay;
But I never saw a man who looked
   So wistfully at the day.

I never saw a man who looked
    With such a wistful eye
Upon that little tent of blue
    Which prisoners call the sky,
And at every drifting cloud that went
    With sails of silver by.

I walked, with other souls in pain,
    Within another ring,
And was wondering if the man had done
    A great or little thing,
When a voice behind me whispered low,
    "That fellow's got to swing."

Dear Christ! the very prison walls
    Suddenly seemed to reel,
And the sky above my head became
    Like a casque of scorching steel;
And, though I was a soul in pain,
    My pain I could not feel.

I only knew what hunted thought
    Quickened his step, and why
He looked upon the garish day
    With such a wistful eye;
The man had killed the thing he loved,
    And so he had to die.

* * * * *

Yet each man kills the thing he loves,
    By each let this be heard,

Some do it with a bitter look,
  Some with a flattering word.
The coward does it with a kiss,
  The brave man with a sword!

Some kill their love when they are young,
  And some when they are old;
Some strangle with the hands of Lust,
  Some with the hands of Gold:
The kindest use a knife, because
  The dead so soon grow cold.

Some love too little, some too long,
  Some sell, and others buy;
Some do the deed with many tears,
  And some without a sigh:
For each man kills the thing he loves,
  Yet each man does not die.

He does not die a death of shame
  On a day of dark disgrace,
Nor have a noose about his neck,
  Nor a cloth upon his face,
Nor drop feet foremost through the floor
  Into an empty space.

He does not sit with silent men
  Who watch him night and day;
Who watch him when he tries to weep,
  And when he tries to pray;
Who watch him lest himself should rob
  The prison of its prey.

He does not wake at dawn to see
	Dread figures throng his room,
The shivering Chaplain robed in white,
	The Sheriff stern with gloom,
And the Governor all in shiny black,
	With the yellow face of Doom.

He does not rise in piteous haste
	To put on convict-clothes,
While some coarse-mouthed Doctor gloats, and notes
	Each new and nerve-twitched pose,
Fingering a watch whose little ticks
	Are like horrible hammer-blows.

He does not feel that sickening thirst
	That sands one's throat, before
The hangman with his gardener's gloves
	Comes through the padded door,
And binds one with three leathern thongs,
	That the throat may thirst no more.

He does not bend his head to hear
	The Burial Office read,
Nor, while the anguish of his soul
	Tells him he is not dead,
Cross his own coffin, as he moves
	Into the hideous shed.

He does not stare upon the air
	Through a little roof of glass:
He does not pray with lips of clay
	For his agony to pass;

Nor feel upon his shuddering cheek
  The kiss of Caiaphas.

II

Six weeks the guardsman walked the yard
  In the suit of shabby grey:
His cricket cap was on his head,
  And his step seemed light and gay,
But I never saw a man who looked
  So wistfully at the day.

I never saw a man who looked
  With such a wistful eye
Upon that little tent of blue
  Which prisoners call the sky,
And at every wandering cloud that trailed
  Its ravelled fleeces by.

He did not wring his hands, as do
  Those witless men who dare
To try to rear the changeling
  In the cave of black Despair:
He only looked upon the sun,
  And drank the morning air.

He did not wring his hands nor weep,
  Nor did he peek or pine,
But he drank the air as though it held
  Some healthful anodyne;
With open mouth he drank the sun
  As though it had been wine!

And I and all the souls in pain,
  Who tramped the other ring,
Forgot if we ourselves had done
  A great or little thing,
And watched with gaze of dull amaze
  The man who had to swing.

For strange it was to see him pass
  With a step so light and gay,
And strange it was to see him look
  So wistfully at the day,
And strange it was to think that he
  Had such a debt to pay.

                * * * * *

For oak and elm have pleasant leaves
  That in the spring-time shoot:
But grim to see is the gallows-tree,
  With its adder-bitten root,
And, green or dry, a man must die
  Before it bears its fruit!

The loftiest place is that seat of grace
  For which all worldlings try:
But who would stand in hempen band
  Upon a scaffold high,
And through a murderer's collar take
  His last look at the sky?

It is sweet to dance to violins
  When Love and Life are fair:

To dance to flutes, to dance to lutes
    Is delicate and rare:
But it is not sweet with nimble feet
    To dance upon the air!

So with curious eyes and sick surmise
    We watched him day by day,
And wondered if each one of us
    Would end the self-same way,
For none can tell to what red Hell
    His sightless soul may stray.

At last the dead man walked no more
    Amongst the Trial Men,
And I knew that he was standing up
    In the black dock's dreadful pen,
And that never would I see his face
    For weal or woe again.

Like two doomed ships that pass in storm
    We had crossed each other's way:
But we made no sign, we said no word,
    We had no word to say;
For we did not meet in the holy night,
    But in the shameful day.

A prison wall was round us both,
    Two outcast men we were:
The world had thrust us from its heart,
    And God from out His care:
And the iron gin that waits for Sin
    Had caught us in its snare.

In Debtors' Yard the stones are hard,
   And the dripping wall is high,
So it was there he took the air
   Beneath the leaden sky,
And by each side a Warder walked,
   For fear the man might die.

Or else he sat with those who watched
   His anguish night and day;
Who watched him when he rose to weep,
   And when he crouched to pray;
Who watched him lest himself should rob
   Their scaffold of its prey.

The Governor was strong upon
   The Regulations Act:
The Doctor said that Death was but
   A scientific fact:
And twice a day the Chaplain called,
   And left a little tract.

And twice a day he smoked his pipe,
   And drank his quart of beer:
His soul was resolute, and held
   No hiding-place for fear;
He often said that he was glad
   The hangman's day was near.

But why he said so strange a thing
   No warder dared to ask:

For he to whom a watcher's doom
   Is given as his task,
Must set a lock upon his lips
   And make his face a mask.

Or else he might be moved, and try
   To comfort or console:
And what should Human Pity do
   Pent up in Murderer's Hole?
What word of grace in such a place
   Could help a brother's soul?

With slouch and swing around the ring
   We trod the Fools' Parade!
We did not care: we knew we were
   The Devil's Own Brigade:
And shaven head and feet of lead
   Make a merry masquerade.

We tore the tarry rope to shreds
   With blunt and bleeding nails;
We rubbed the doors, and scrubbed the floors,
   And cleaned the shining rails:
And, rank by rank, we soaped the plank,
   And clattered with the pails.

We sewed the sacks, we broke the stones,
   We turned the dusty drill:
We banged the tins, and bawled the hymns,
   And sweated on the mill:
But in the heart of every man
   Terror was lying still.

So still it lay that every day
    Crawled like a weed-clogged wave:
And we forgot the bitter lot
    That waits for fool and knave,
Till once, as we tramped in from work,
    We passed an open grave.

With yawning mouth the yellow hole
    Gaped for a living thing;
The very mud cried out for blood
    To the thirsty asphalte ring:
And we knew that ere one dawn grew fair
    Some prisoner had to swing.

Right in we went, with soul intent
    On Death and Dread and Doom:
The hangman, with his little bag,
    Went shuffling through the gloom:
And I trembled as I groped my way
    Into my numbered tomb.

* * * * *

That night the empty corridors
    Were full of forms of Fear,
And up and down the iron town
    Stole feet we could not hear,
And through the bars that hide the stars
    White faces seemed to peer.

He lay as one who lies and dreams
    In a pleasant meadow-land,

The watchers watched him as he slept,
    And could not understand
How one could sleep so sweet a sleep
    With a hangman close at hand.

But there is no sleep when men must weep
    Who never yet have wept:
So we—the fool, the fraud, the knave—
    That endless vigil kept,
And through each brain on hands of pain
    Another's terror crept.

Alas! it is a fearful thing
    To feel another's guilt!
For, right, within, the Sword of Sin
    Pierced to its poisoned hilt,
And as molten lead were the tears we shed
    For the blood we had not spilt.

The warders with their shoes of felt
    Crept by each padlocked door,
And peeped and saw, with eyes of awe,
    Grey figures on the floor,
And wondered why men knelt to pray
    Who never prayed before.

All through the night we knelt and prayed,
    Mad mourners of a corse!
The troubled plumes of midnight shook
    The plumes upon a hearse:
And bitter wine upon a sponge
    Was the savour of Remorse.

The grey cock crew, the red cock crew,
    But never came the day:
And crooked shapes of Terror crouched,
    In the corners where we lay:
And each evil sprite that walks by night
    Before us seemed to play.

They glided past, they glided fast,
    Like travellers through a mist:
They mocked the moon in a rigadoon
    Of delicate turn and twist,
And with formal pace and loathsome grace
    The phantoms kept their tryst.

With mop and mow, we saw them go,
    Slim shadows hand in hand:
About, about, in ghostly rout
    They trod a saraband:
And the damned grotesques made arabesques,
    Like the wind upon the sand!

With the pirouettes of marionettes,
    They tripped on pointed tread:
But with flutes of Fear they filled the ear,
    As their grisly masque they led,
And loud they sang, and long they sang,
    For they sang to wake the dead.

"Oho!" they cried, "The world is wide,
    But fettered limbs go lame!

And once, or twice, to throw the dice
  Is a gentlemanly game,
But he does not win who plays with Sin
  In the secret House of Shame."

No things of air these antics were,
  That frolicked with such glee:
To men whose lives were held in gyves,
  And whose feet might not go free,
Ah! wounds of Christ! they were living things,
  Most terrible to see.

Around, around, they waltzed and wound;
  Some wheeled in smirking pairs;
With the mincing step of a demirep
  Some sidled up the stairs:
And with subtle sneer, and fawning leer,
  Each helped us at our prayers.

The morning wind began to moan,
  But still the night went on:
Through its giant loom the web of gloom
  Crept till each thread was spun:
And, as we prayed, we grew afraid
  Of the Justice of the Sun.

The moaning wind went wandering round
  The weeping prison-wall:
Till like a wheel of turning steel
  We felt the minutes crawl:
O moaning wind! what had we done
  To have such a seneschal?

At last I saw the shadowed bars,
    Like a lattice wrought in lead,
Move right across the whitewashed wall
    That faced my three-plank bed,
And I knew that somewhere in the world
    God's dreadful dawn was red.

At six o'clock we cleaned our cells,
    At seven all was still,
But the sough and swing of a mighty wing
    The prison seemed to fill,
For the Lord of Death with icy breath
    Had entered in to kill.

He did not pass in purple pomp,
    Nor ride a moon-white steed.
Three yards of cord and a sliding board
    Are all the gallows' need:
So with rope of shame the Herald came
    To do the secret deed.

We were as men who through a fen
    Of filthy darkness grope:
We did not dare to breathe a prayer,
    Or to give our anguish scope:
Something was dead in each of us,
    And what was dead was Hope.

For Man's grim Justice goes its way,
    And will not swerve aside:
It slays the weak, it slays the strong,
    It has a deadly stride:

With iron heel it slays the strong,
    The monstrous parricide!

We waited for the stroke of eight:
    Each tongue was thick with thirst:
For the stroke of eight is the stroke of Fate
    That makes a man accursed,
And Fate will use a running noose
    For the best man and the worst.

We had no other thing to do,
    Save to wait for the sign to come:
So, like things of stone in a valley lone,
    Quiet we sat and dumb:
But each man's heart beat thick and quick,
    Like a madman on a drum!

With sudden shock the prison-clock
    Smote on the shivering air,
And from all the gaol rose up a wail
    Of impotent despair,
Like the sound that frightened marches hear
    From some leper in his lair.

And as one sees most fearful things
    In the crystal of a dream,
We saw the greasy hempen rope
    Hooked to the blackened beam,
And heard the prayer the hangman's snare
    Strangled into a scream.

And all the woe that moved him so
    That he gave that bitter cry,
And the wild regrets, and the bloody sweats,
    None knew so well as I:
For he who lives more lives than one
    More deaths than one must die.

IV

There is no chapel on the day
    On which they hang a man:
The Chaplain's heart is far too sick,
    Or his face is far too wan,
Or there is that written in his eyes
    Which none should look upon.

So they kept us close till nigh on noon,
    And then they rang the bell,
And the warders with their jingling keys
    Opened each listening cell,
And down the iron stair we tramped,
    Each from his separate Hell.

Out into God's sweet air we went,
    But not in wonted way,
For this man's face was white with fear,
    And that man's face was grey,
And I never saw sad men who looked
    So wistfully at the day.

I never saw sad men who looked
    With such a wistful eye

Upon that little tent of blue
    We prisoners called the sky,
And at every happy cloud that passed
    In such strange freedom by.

But there were those amongst us all
    Who walked with downcast head,
And knew that, had each got his due,
    They should have died instead:
He had but killed a thing that lived,
    Whilst they had killed the dead.

For he who sins a second time
    Wakes a dead soul to pain,
And draws it from its spotted shroud,
    And makes it bleed again,
And makes it bleed great gouts of blood,
    And makes it bleed in vain!

                    * * * * *

Like ape or clown, in monstrous garb
    With crooked arrows starred,
Silently we went round and round
    The slippery asphalte yard;
Silently we went round and round,
    And no man spoke a word.

Silently we went round and round,
    And through each hollow mind
The Memory of dreadful things
    Rushed like a dreadful wind,

And Horror stalked before each man,
  And Terror crept behind.

* * * * *

The warders strutted up and down,
  And watched their herd of brutes,
Their uniforms were spick and span,
  And they wore their Sunday suits,
But we knew the work they had been at,
  By the quicklime on their boots.

For where a grave had opened wide,
  There was no grave at all:
Only a stretch of mud and sand
  By the hideous prison-wall,
And a little heap of burning lime,
  That the man should have his pall.

For he has a pall, this wretched man,
  Such as few men can claim:
Deep down below a prison-yard,
  Naked for greater shame,
He lies, with fetters on each foot,
  Wrapt in a sheet of flame!

And all the while the burning lime
  Eats flesh and bone away,
It eats the brittle bone by night,
  And the soft flesh by day,
It eats the flesh and bone by turns,
  But it eats the heart alway.

For three long years they will not sow
    Or root or seedling there:
For three long years the unblessed spot
    Will sterile be and bare,
And look upon the wondering sky
    With unreproachful stare.

They think a murderer's heart would taint
    Each simple seed they sow.
It is not true! God's kindly earth
    Is kindlier than men know,
And the red rose would but blow more red,
    The white rose whiter blow.

Out of his mouth a red, red rose!
    Out of his heart a white!
For who can say by what strange way,
    Christ brings His will to light,
Since the barren staff the pilgrim bore
    Bloomed in the great Pope's sight?

But neither milk-white rose nor red
    May bloom in prison-air;
The shard, the pebble, and the flint,
    Are what they give us there:
For flowers have been known to heal
    A common man's despair.

So never will wine-red rose or white,
    Petal by petal, fall

On that stretch of mud and sand that lies
   By the hideous prison-wall,
To tell the men who tramp the yard
   That God's Son died for all.

Yet though the hideous prison-wall
   Still hems him round and round,
And a spirit may not walk by night
   That is with fetters bound,
And a spirit may but weep that lies
   In such unholy ground.

He is at peace-this wretched man—
   At peace, or will be soon:
There is no thing to make him mad,
   Nor does Terror walk at noon,
For the lampless Earth in which he lies
   Has neither Sun nor Moon.

They hanged him as a beast is hanged:
   They did not even toll
A requiem that might have brought
   Rest to his startled soul,
But hurriedly they took him out,
   And hid him in a hole.

The warders stripped him of his clothes,
   And gave him to the flies:
They mocked the swollen purple throat,
   And the stark and staring eyes:
And with laughter loud they heaped the shroud
   In which the convict lies.

The Chaplain would not kneel to pray
    By his dishonoured grave:
Nor mark it with that blessed Cross
    That Christ for sinners gave,
Because the man was one of those
    Whom Christ came down to save.

Yet all is well; he has but passed
    To Life's appointed bourne:
And alien tears will fill for him
    Pity's long-broken urn,
For his mourners will be outcast men,
    And outcasts always mourn.

V

I know not whether Laws be right,
    Or whether Laws be wrong;
All that we know who lie in gaol
    Is that the wall is strong;
And that each day is like a year,
    A year whose days are long.

But this I know, that every Law
    That men have made for Man,
Since first Man took his brother's life,
    And the sad world began,
But straws the wheat and saves the chaff
    With a most evil fan.

This too I know—and wise it were
    If each could know the same—

That every prison that men build
   Is built with bricks of shame,
And bound with bars lest Christ should see
   How men their brothers maim.

With bars they blur the gracious moon,
   And blind the goodly sun:
And they do well to hide their Hell,
   For in it things are done
That Son of God nor son of Man
   Ever should look upon!

* * * * *

The vilest deeds like poison weeds,
   Bloom well in prison-air;
It is only what is good in Man
   That wastes and withers there:
Pale Anguish keeps the heavy gate,
   And the Warder is Despair.

For they starve the little frightened child
   Till it weeps both night and day:
And they scourge the weak, and flog the fool,
   And gibe the old and grey,
And some grow mad, and all grow bad,
   And none a word may say.

Each narrow cell in which we dwell
   Is a foul and dark latrine,
And the fetid breath of living Death
   Chokes up each grated screen,

And all, but Lust, is turned to dust
   In humanity's machine.

The brackish water that we drink
Creeps with a loathsome slime,
And the bitter bread they weigh in scales
Is full of chalk and lime,
And Sleep will not lie down, but walks
Wild-eyed, and cries to Time.

*   *   *   *   *

But though lean Hunger and green Thirst
Like asp with adder fight,
We have little care of prison fare,
For what chills and kills outright
Is that every stone one lifts by day
Becomes one's heart by night.

With midnight always in one's heart,
And twilight in one's cell,
We turn the crank, or tear the rope,
Each in his separate Hell,
And the silence is more awful far
Than the sound of a brazen bell.

And never a human voice comes near
To speak a gentle word:
And the eye that watches through the door
Is pitiless and hard:
And by all forgot, we rot and rot,
With soul and body marred.

And thus we rust Life's iron chain
Degraded and alone:
And some men curse and some men weep,
   And some men make no moan:
But God's eternal Laws are kind
   And break the heart of stone.

And every human heart that breaks,
   In prison-cell or yard,
Is as that broken box that gave
   Its treasure to the Lord,
And filled the unclean leper's house
   With the scent of costliest nard.

Ah! happy they whose hearts can break
   And peace of pardon win!
How else man may make straight his plan
   And cleanse his soul from Sin?
How else but through a broken heart
   May Lord Christ enter in?

* * * * *

And he of the swollen purple throat,
   And the stark and staring eyes,
Waits for the holy hands that took
   The Thief to Paradise;
And a broken and a contrite heart
   The Lord will not despise.

The man in red who reads the Law
   Gave him three weeks of life,
Three little weeks in which to heal His soul of his soul's strife,

And cleanse from every blot of blood
   The hand that held the knife.

And with tears of blood he cleansed the hand,
   The hand that held the steel:
For only blood can wipe out blood,
   And only tears can heal:
And the crimson stain that was of Cain
   Became Christ's snow-white seal.

VI

In Reading gaol by Reading town
   There is a pit of shame,
And in it lies a wretched man
   Eaten by teeth of flame,
In a burning winding-sheet he lies,
   And his grave has got no name.

And there, till Christ call forth the dead,
   In silence let him lie:
No need to waste the foolish tear,
   Or heave the windy sigh:
The man had killed the thing he loved,
   And so he had to die.

And all men kill the thing they love,
   By all let this be heard,
Some do it with a bitter look,
   Some with a flattering word,
The coward does it with a kiss,
   The brave man with a sword!

APPENDIX

From "Percy's Reliques"—Volume I.

THE FROLICKSOME DUKE

Printed from a black-letter copy in the Pepys Collection.

KING ESTMERE

This ballad is given from two versions, one in the Percy folio manuscript, and of considerable antiquity. The original version was probably written at the end of the fifteenth century.

ROBIN HOOD AND GUY OF GISBORNE

One of the earliest known ballads about Robin Hood—from the Percy folio manuscript.

KING COPHETUA AND THE BEGGAR MAID

This ballad is printed from Richard Johnson's *Crown Garland of Goulden Roses,* 1612.

THE FRIAR OF ORDERS GRAY

This ballad is composed of innumerable small fragments of ancient ballads found throughout the plays of Shakespeare, which Thomas Percy formed into one.

SIR ALDINGAR

Given from the Percy folio manuscript, with some additional stanzas added by Thomas Percy to complete the story.

EDOM O'GORDON

A Scottish ballad—this version was printed at Glasgow in 1755 by Robert and Andrew Foulis. It has been enlarged with several stanzas, recovered from a fragment of the same ballad, from the Percy folio manuscript.

THE BALLAD OF CHEVY CHACE

From the Percy folio manuscript, amended by two or three others printed in black-letter. Written about the time of Elizabeth.

SIR LANCELOT DU LAKE

Given from a printed copy, corrected in part by an extract from the Percy folio manuscript.

THE CHILD OF ELLE

Partly from the Percy folio manuscript, with several additional stanzas by Percy as the original copy was defective and mutilated.

KING EDWARD IV AND THE TANNER OF TAM WORTH

The text in this ballad is selected from two copies in black-letter. One in the Bodleian Library, printed at London by John Danter in 1596. The other copy, without date, is from the Pepys Collection.

SIR PATRICK SPENS

Printed from two manuscript copies transmitted from Scotland. It is possible that this ballad is founded on historical fact.

EDWARD, EDWARD

An old Scottish ballad—from a manuscript copy transmitted from Scotland.

KING LEIR AND HIS THREE DAUGHTERS

Version from an old copy in the *Golden Garland,* black-letter, entitled *A lamentable Song of the Death of King Lear and his Three Daughters.*

THE GABERLUNZIE MAN

This ballad is said to have been written by King James V of Scotland.

From "Percy's Reliques"—Volume II.

THE KNIGHT AND SHEPHERD'S DAUGHTER

Printed from an old black-letter copy, with some corrections.

KING JOHN AND THE ABBOT OF CANTERBURY

This ballad was abridged and modernized in the time of James I from one much older, entitled *King John and the Bishop of Canterbury.* The version given here is from an ancient black-letter copy.

BARBARA ALLEN'S CRUELTY

Given, with some corrections, from an old black-letter copy, entitled *Barbara Alien's Cruelty, or the Young Man's Tragedy.*

FAIR ROSAMOND

The version of this ballad given here is from four ancient copies in black-letter: two of them in the Pepys' Library. It is by Thomas Delone. First printed in 1612.

THE BOY AND THE MANTLE

This is a revised and modernized version of a very old ballad.

THE HEIR OF LINNE

Given from the Percy folio manuscript, with several additional stanzas supplied by Thomas Percy.

SIR ANDREW BARTON

This ballad is from the Percy folio manuscript with additions and amendments from an ancient black-letter copy in the Pepys' Collection. It was written probably at the end of the sixteenth century.

THE BEGGAR'S DAUGHTER OF BEDNALL GREEN

Given from the Percy folio manuscript, with a few additions and alterations from two ancient printed copies.

BRAVE LORD WILLOUGHBEY

Given from an old black-letter copy.

THE SPANISH LADY'S LOVE

The version of an ancient black-letter copy, edited in part from the Percy folio manuscript.

GIL MORRICE

The version of this ballad given here was printed at Glasgow in 1755. Since this date sixteen additional verses have been discovered and added to the original ballad.

CHILD WATERS

From the Percy folio manuscript, with corrections.

THE BAILIFF'S DAUGHTER OF ISLINGTON

From an ancient black-letter copy in the Pepys' Collection.

THE LYE

By Sir Walter Raleigh. This poem is from a scarce miscellany entitled *Davison's Poems, or a poeticall Rapsodie divided into sixe books . . . the 4th impression newly corrected and augmented and put into a forme more pleasing to the reader.* Lond. 1621.

From "English and Scottish Ballads."

MAY COLLIN

From a manuscript at Abbotsford in the Sir Walter Scott Collection, *Scotch Ballads, Materials for Border Minstrelsy.*

THOMAS THE RHYMER

Scotch Ballads, Materials for Border Minstrelsy, No. 97, Abbotsford. From the Sir Walter Scott Collection. Communicated to Sir Walter by Mrs. Christiana Greenwood, London, May 27th, 1806.

YOUNG BEICHAN

Taken from the Jamieson-Brown manuscript, 1783.

CLERK COLVILL

From a transcript of No. 13 of William Tytler's Brown manuscript.

THE EARL OF MAR'S DAUGHTER

From Buchan's *Ballads of the North of Scotland,* 1828.

HYND HORN

From Motherwell's manuscript, 1825 and after.

THE THREE RAVENS

Melismate. Musicall Phansies. Fitting the Court, Cittie and Country Humours. London, 1611. (T. Ravenscroft.)

THE WIFE OF USHER'S WELL

Printed from *Ministrelsy of the Scottish Border*, 1802.

* * * * *

MANDALAY
By Rudyard Kipling.

JOHN BROWN'S BODY

IT'S A LONG WAY TO TIPPERARY
By Jack Judge and Harry Williams.

THE BALLAD OF READING GAOL
By Oscar Wilde.

9 781297 061462